Pieter,

Thought it was about time you had something on your namesake in your collection! Looking forward to the day you can show it to me in the flesh.

All my love

XXXX...etc.

Jan 2000

ST. PETER'S

ST. PETER

ST. PETER'S
ST. PETER

Photographs/Fotografien AURELIO AMENDOLA

Text BRUNO CONTARDI

Foreword/Vorwort VIRGILIO CARD. NOÈ

Archpriest of the Basilica St. Peter's, President of the Fabbrica of St. Peter's
Erzpriester der Basilika von St. Peter, Präsident der Bauhütte von St. Peter

teNeues

Our most heartfelt thanks to Alfredo Maria Pergolizzi for his willingness to help and invaluable assistance.

I would like to express my thanks to Francesca Amendola for her constructive and indispensable contribution to the production of this volume (a. a.).

We extend our thanks to the following institutions for reproductions illustrating the text:
Staatliche Museen Preussischer Kulturbesitz, Kupferstichkabinett, Berlin; Palais des Beaux-arts, Collection Wicar, Lille; Teylers Museum, Haarlem; Graphische Sammlung Albertina, Vienna; Pierpont Morgan Library, New York.

Photographic Acknowledgements:
Jörg P. Anders, Berlin; Fototeca Biblioteca Hertziana, Rome; Gabinetto fotografico, Soprintendenza per i Beni Artistici e Storici, Rome; Gabinetto Disegni e Stampe, Uffizi, Florence.

Besonderer Dank gilt Alfredo Maria Pergolizzi für seine Disponibilität und wertvolle Zusammenarbeit.

Ich möchte Francesca Amendola meinen Dank für ihre tatkräftige und unentbehrliche Mitarbeit bei der Verwirklichung dieses Bandes aussprechen (a. a.).

Für die Abbildungen zum Text möchten wir den folgenden Institutionen danken:
Staatliche Museen Preussischer Kulturbesitz, Kupferstichkabinett, Berlin; Palais des Beaux-arts, Collection Wicar, Lille; Teylers Museum, Haarlem; Graphische Sammlung Albertina, Wien; Pierpont Morgan Library, New York.

Fotografische Beiträge:
Jörg P. Anders, Berlin; Fototeca Biblioteca Hertziana, Rom; Gabinetto fotografico, Soprintendenza per i Beni Artistici e Storici, Rom; Gabinetto Disegni e Stampe, Uffizien, Florenz.

For this edition:
© 1999 te Neues Verlag GmbH, Kempen
For the original edition:
© 1998 Federico Motta Editore S.p.A., Milan
For the photographs:
© 1998 Aurelio Amendola

Original book title: Aurelio Amendola, San Pietro

Production: Christiane Blass, Cologne
English translation: Clarice Zdanski
German translation: Beate Baumann Giacobbe, Messina
German editing: Susanne Klinkhamels, Cologne

ISBN 3–8238–0961–X (English cover)
ISBN 3–8238–0542–8 (German cover)
Printed in Italy

The basilica St. Peter's on the Vatican, a meeting place of different artistic forms and experiences, is among the most voluminously studied and described religious buildings, owing to its extensive bibliography. Almost as an accompaniment to the slow development of critical thought on the part of art historians, the greatest temple of Christianity has been presented in its most varied aspects: from specialist publications, popular books, and guides, to manuals. In every period, the written work has been accompanied by images, and, even if today there is still no complete anthology, who has not happened to come across – at least once – one of the numerous engravings which represents the perspectival views of the central nave, the most well-known and best loved monuments, the accounts of the most important or most significant liturgical events? The visual history of this monument has never been lacking throughout the course of time. Even though passing trends have characterized different periods of art, artists have never stopped celebrating the colors and the luminous hues of the vast internal spaces of the basilica, creating, especially in the nineteenth century, magical atmospheres animated by the characteristic presence of the Roman people. In our century, the coming of photography should have rung in a new, more enduring history of images of the basilica St. Peter's, but this has not come about. Amidst an infinity of images, which soon tire the reader in the descriptive duplication of monuments, there have been few visual records which go beyond simple documentation, and revitalize, in a new sort of artistic exegesis, the countless ideas offered by the whole. A very interesting work is presented here, and it is the fruit of the experience and, above all, the artistic sensitivity of Aurelio Amendola: he captures the atmosphere so often praised by visitors from every age, when natural light was the only guide. As Aurelio Amendola moves around in the Vatican basilica, he is inspired and attracted by every little part, alone among the immense spaces. His artistic taste has caused him to be interested both in the monument as well as the simple decoration of a pier or a pilaster, with the same intensity. In imparting an autonomous value to every single part, Amendola suggests a modern reading of the basilica, and with patience and fortunate intuition, he brings together different styles and forms, without letting himself be taken in by esthetic biases or academic superiority. His photographic lens searches for new aspects inside the works, and a look, a detail, a glimpse, is inserted among the pages of this volume with forceful autonomy. A new, original guide, then, which will surely fascinate and arouse the curiosity of whoever thinks he might have seen all of the basilica of St. Peter's up to now.

Virgilio Card. Noè
Archpriest of the Basilica St. Peter's
President of the Fabbrica of St. Peter's

Die Basilika von Sankt Peter im Vatikan, in der unterschiedliche künstlerische Formen und Erfahrungen zusammenfließen, gehört aufgrund des umfangreichen bibliographischen Materials zu den am meisten beschriebenen und untersuchten kirchlichen Bauwerken. Gleichsam als ob dem langsamen Fortschreiten der kritischen Beobachtungen der Kunsthistoriker Folge geleistet werden sollte, wurde der bedeutendste Kultort der Christenheit auf unterschiedlichste Weise untersucht, in fachwissenschaftlichen Veröffentlichungen und volkstümlichen Sammlungen, in Führern und Handbüchern. In jeder Epoche wurde das geschriebene Wort von Bildern begleitet, und dennoch existierte bis heute keine vollständige Zusammenstellung. Aber wer ist nicht mindestens einmal auf einen der zahlreichen Stiche gestoßen, auf denen die perspektivischen Ansichten des Mittelschiffs, die bekanntesten und beliebtesten Kunstwerke und die Zeugnisse der wichtigsten und bedeutendsten liturgischen Ereignisse dargestellt sind? Der sichtbare Erfolg dieses Bauwerks hat im Laufe der Zeit nie nachgelassen. Auf der Spur neuer Tendenzen, die die verschiedenen künstlerischen Epochen kennzeichneten, hat man niemals aufgehört, die Farben und die leuchtenden Töne des weiten Innenraums der Basilika zu rühmen; insbesondere im 19. Jahrhundert wurde eine bezaubernde Atmosphäre geschaffen, die durch die charakteristische Anwesenheit der Römer zusätzlich belebt wurde. In unserem Jahrhundert ließ der Einzug der Fotografie einen neuen, dauerhafteren Erfolg der Bilder der Peterskirche erahnen, was sich jedoch nicht bewahrheitet hat. Unter den unendlich zahlreichen Aufnahmen, die sich auf eine beschreibende Wiedergabe beschränkten, waren nur wenige visuelle Zeugnisse, die über eine einfache Darstellung hinausgingen und die unzähligen Anregungen, die das Gesamtbild bietet, künstlerisch neu interpretierten. Einen hochinteressanten Vorschlag macht Aurelio Amendola, der sich durch seine Erfahrung und insbesondere durch seine künstlerische Sensibilität auszeichnet. Er fängt die Atmosphäre ein, die die Besucher zu jeder Zeit, als das Sonnenlicht ihr einziger Führer war, so sehr bezauberte. Aurelio Amendola bewegt sich allein in der gewaltigen Weite der Vatikanbasilika, wobei er sich von jedem Detail inspirieren und anziehen läßt. Sein künstlerischer Geschmack bewirkt sein gleich starkes Interesse an einem bekannten Kunstwerk und einer einfachen Pfeiler- oder Lisenendekoration. Indem Amendola jedem einzelnen Element einen eigenen Wert beimißt, legt er mit Geduld und gelungener Intuition eine moderne Sichtweise der Basilika nahe und rückt unterschiedliche Formen und Stile aneinander, ohne sich dabei von ästhetischen Vorurteilen oder akademischen Vorrangstellungen künstlerischer Überlegenheit beeinflussen zu lassen. Sein Objektiv sucht innerhalb der Werke neue Aspekte; ein Blick, ein Detail und ein Ausschnitt fügen sich mit eindringlicher Selbständigkeit in die Seiten dieses Bandes ein. Ein neuer, origineller Führer also, der sicherlich Faszination und Neugierde auch bei denjenigen weckt, die bislang davon überzeugt waren, alles in der Peterskirche gesehen zu haben.

Virgilio Card. Noè
Erzpriester der Basilika von St. Peter
Präsident der Bauhütte von St. Peter

"Tu es Petrus"

To the students of History of Architecture II in Ferrara

Bruno Contardi

As Bishop of Rome, the pontiff's seat is the basilica of St. John Lateran, the cathedral of the Urbe, founded by Constantine in the winter of 312/313, immediately after the Battle of the Milvian Bridge (28 October, 312), that marked both the defeat of his rival Maxentius, and the official recognition of Christianity on the part of the new emperor. Constantine himself donated the area, which belonged to the imperial domain (in fact, the barracks for the cavalry which had fought at Maxentius' side had stood there), and took on the burden of constructing what was to become the first Christian public building. The following structures were next to the basilica of St. John Lateran: the baptistery (probably built in 315), the residence of the bishop of Rome – also called the patriarchate – and, later, a series of buildings of extraordinary importance. They constituted a true pontifical citadel, which was both the seat of spiritual power, and from the fifth century onwards, of the temporal administration of the Urbe.

But the motive for recognizing the Bishop of Rome's supremacy within the Church, or the role of Universal Shepherd, is that the person of the pontiff is the successor of St. Peter, the humble fisherman of Galilee whom Christ himself chose as prince of the Apostles, changing his name from Simon to Peter, the rock upon which he would found his Church. "Tu es Petrus et super hanc petram aedificabo Ecclesiam meam et tibi dabo claves Regni Caelorum": the passage in the Gospel on which the historical pretext of the supremacy of the successor is based is still read in the most conspicuous place in the basilica, at the base of the dome. Following what he felt as a calling, St. Peter came from Galilee to Rome to preach the new faith in the very capital of the Empire, and there, in the year 64 of the Christian era, he was martyred and buried together with St. Paul. On the Vatican hill, in the second century, a small, modest shrine was constructed on the tomb of the first among the Apostles, in a cemetery of sumptuous pagan mausoleums. What remains of it, already referred to as the "trophy of St. Peter" around 200 as a symbol of victory at the death of the first pontiff, was discovered about fifty years ago. Between 319 and 322, Constantine wanted to build an enormous church commemorating Peter; it was finished in 329. Since it was essentially a huge embankment constructed by filling in the pagan necropolis, it was different from other contemporary churches constructed in memory of various famous martyrs (like St. Lawrence or St. Agnes) in that the building did not stand in the vicinity of a catacomb, but directly on the burial place. And the upper part of the aedicule which showed where the tomb of the apostle was remained above the level of the floor of the Constantinian basilica, at the crossing of the transept – where the five great naves came together – with the apse. The shrine of the apostle was surmounted by a

„Tu es Petrus"

Den Studenten des Lehrstuhls Architekturgeschichte II in Ferrara

Bruno Contardi

Als Bischof von Rom hat der Papst seinen Sitz in der Basilika San Giovanni in Laterano, der Kathedrale Roms. Gegründet wurde die Lateranbasilika von Konstantin d. Gr. im Winter 312/313, unmittelbar nach der Schlacht an der Milvischen Brücke (28. Oktober 312), die nicht nur die Niederlage seines Rivalen Maxentius besiegelte, sondern gleichzeitig die offizielle Legitimation des Christentums durch den neuen Kaiser darstellte. Das Gebiet, das zum kaiserlichen Besitz gehörte (hier befanden sich die Kasernen der Reitergarde, die auf Maxentius' Seite gekämpft hatte), überließ Konstantin als persönliches Geschenk. Der Kaiser ließ auch das erste öffentliche christliche Bauwerk errichten. Neben der Basilika San Giovanni in Laterano entstanden das Baptisterium (vermutlich im Jahr 315) und die Residenz des römischen Bischofs, auch „Patriarchio" (Patriarchensitz) genannt. In späterer Zeit kamen weitere Bauten von außerordentlicher Bedeutung hinzu, so daß eine regelrechte päpstliche Zitadelle entstand, die Sitz der geistlichen Macht und seit dem 5. Jahrhundert auch der kirchlichen Verwaltung der Hauptstadt war.

Der Grund jedoch, weshalb dem Bischof von Rom die Vorherrschaft innerhalb der Kirche, die Rolle des universellen Hirten, zuerkannt wird, ist die Tatsache, daß der Papst als der Nachfolger des hl. Petrus gilt, des einfachen Fischers aus Galiläa, den Christus selbst als Apostelfürsten erwählt hatte und dessen Namen er von Simon zu Petrus abwandelte, der Fels, auf dem die Kirche errichtet werden sollte. „Tu es Petrus et super hanc petram aedificabo Ecclesiam meam et tibi dabo claves Regni Caelorum": Dieser Passus des Evangeliums, auf dem die Suprematie des Nachfolgers des hl. Petrus beruht, ist auch heute noch an der wichtigsten Stelle der Basilika, am unteren Rand der Kuppel, zu lesen. Seiner Berufung folgend, kam der hl. Petrus von Galiläa nach Rom, um den neuen Glauben in der Hauptstadt des Reiches selbst zu verbreiten; hier wurde er 64 n. Chr. zusammen mit dem hl. Paulus als Märtyrer hingerichtet und begraben. Auf dem Vatikanhügel hatte man im 2. Jahrhundert über dem Grab des Apostelfürsten, inmitten eines aus prächtigen heidnischen Mausoleen bestehenden Friedhofs, ein kleines, bescheidenes Heiligtum errichtet, dessen Überreste vor ca. 50 Jahren entdeckt wurden. Schon um das Jahr 200 wurde es als „Trophäe des hl. Petrus" bezeichnet, ein Symbol für den Sieg des ersten Papstes über den Tod. Zwischen 319 und 322 ließ Konstantin auf der Gedenkstätte des hl. Petrus eine große Kirche errichten, die 329 vollendet wurde. Sie wurde durch die Aufschüttung einer heidnischen Nekropole auf einem großen Erdwall erbaut und befand sich im Unterschied zu anderen zeitgenössischen Kirchen, die zum Gedenken an berühmte Märtyrer entstanden waren (wie San Lorenzo oder Sant'Agnese), nicht in der Nähe einer Katakombe, sondern unmittelbar am Bestattungsort. Am Kreuzungspunkt des Querschiffs, das die fünf großen

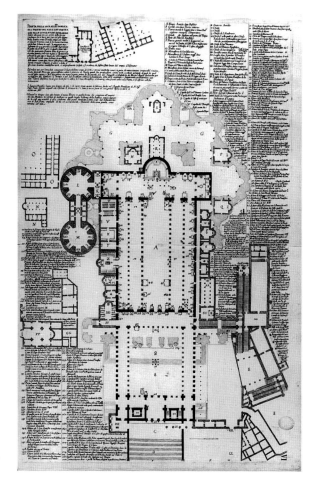

Plan of the ancient basilica of St. Peter's with the plan of the present basilica superimposed, in Tiberio Alfarano, *De Basilicae Vaticanae antiquissima et nova structura*, Rome 1571, tav. 6

Grundriß der alten Peterskirche mit darüberliegendem Grundriß der heutigen Basilika, aus: Tiberio Alfarano, *De Basilicae Vaticanae antiquissima et nova structura*, Rom 1571, Tafel 6

ciborium, and later, in the sixth century, a semicircular corridor allowed the crowds of faithful who came from all over Europe to offer gifts, pray and implore Christ's successor on earth for eternal salvation.

Throughout the entire period of the Middle Ages, conflict and heated rivalry had developed between St. John Lateran – a visible demonstration of the victory over paganism – and St. Peter on the Vatican – not only as a place of popular devotion, but also as a source of authority for the Roman pontiff. The Vatican basilica won out, with its progressive accentuation of pontifical power and its independence from the Eastern Empire. In fact, for the Roman pontiff, to emphasize the relationship of contiguity and continuity with the successor of the Son of God meant nothing other than claiming his own supremacy within the universal Church. Thus, it is not surprising to find the basilica at the center of all events – not only religious, but also purely political – for the entire first Christian milennium. This marked the gradual affirmation of the papacy as the entity which also had temporal power – including the coronation of emperors, first the Carolingians, then the Ottonians, and finally the Germanic emperors – a symbol of the recognized submission of the new imperial power to pontifical power.

The different polarity of the two churches was above all historical and ideological, and, in the end, was emphasized by their different urban locations. The first church had been placed within the Aurelian walls, but in an area, the Lateran, which was difficult to defend from a military point of view. There were also problems with the water supply as the ancient aqueducts fell into ruins, and so the area came to be abandoned by the urban population. Instead, the second church was on the other side of the river, hence outside the ancient inhabited area, but it was soon capable of organizing around itself a citadel, the Borgo, in every sense of the word. Walls were built around it in the ninth century, and the only point of access – the ancient Pons Aelius, the present Ponte degli Angeli – could easily be defended once Castel Sant'Angelo, the tomb of the imperial family erected by Hadrian in the second century and transformed into an impregnable stronghold, had been taken control of. The dominance of St. Peter's over the Lateran basilica was finally established, from the first years of the thirteenth century on, by the construction of a palatial residence beside the church. It was later enlarged, and became the papal see.

Julius II's decision (pope from 1503 to 1513) at the beginning of his pontificate to demolish the thousand-year-old church in order to construct a new St. Peter's with a modern plan from the foundations up was not along the order of purely esthetic considerations, since the historical, ideological and religious importance connected with the basilica was so great. Certainly, the great nave must have presented static imbalances which could not be ignored; and the irregular sequence of chapels, oratories, altars and tombs must have ruined the original simplicity of the scheme, since it could not but seem haphazard and disorderly. The space of the apse by that

Längsschiffe abschloß, mit der Apsis war sogar der obere Teil der Ädikula zu sehen, die über die Fußbodenebene der konstantinischen Basilika hinausragte und auf das Apostelgrab hinwies. Über dem Heiligtum des Apostels erhob sich ein Ziborium; ein halbrunder Gang, der im 6. Jahrhundert angefügt wurde, ermöglichte den zahlreichen Gläubigen, die aus allen Teilen des westlichen Europas anreisten, um Geschenke darzubringen, zu beten und den Nachfolger Christi auf Erden um Rettung anzuflehen, die Sicht auf die Grabstätte.

Zwischen San Giovanni in Laterano, dem sichtbaren Beweis des Sieges über das Heidentum, und San Pietro in Vaticano, nicht nur ein Ort der Hingabe des Volkes, sondern auch Autoritätsquelle des römischen Papstes, entbrannte das ganze Mittelalter hindurch ein Konflikt und heftige Rivalität. Infolge der schrittweisen Stärkung der päpstlichen Machtstellung und deren zunehmender Eigenständigkeit gegenüber dem Ostreich war die Vatikanbasilika überlegen. Für den römischen Papst bedeutete die Betonung der Kontiguität und Kontinuität mit dem Nachfolger in erster Linie den Anspruch auf die eigene Vorherrschaft innerhalb der Universalkirche. Es verwundert daher nicht, daß die Basilika im gesamten ersten christlichen Jahrtausend im Mittelpunkt nicht nur religiöser, sondern auch ausgesprochen politischer Ereignisse stand. So behauptete sich das Papsttum allmählich als eine Institution, die auch weltliche Macht ausübte, wie beispielsweise bei den Kaiserkrönungen der Karolinger, Ottonen und deutschen Herrscher, die die Anerkennung der Unterwerfung der neuen kaiserlichen Macht unter die päpstliche Macht symbolisierte.

Die verschiedenartige, insbesondere historische und ideologische Polarität der beiden Kirchen kam schließlich auch durch ihre unterschiedliche Lage in der Stadt zum Ausdruck. Die Lateranbasilika lag innerhalb des aurelianischen Stadtmauerrings; allerdings war das Laterangebiet militärisch nur schwer zu verteidigen und wies Probleme hinsichtlich der Wasserversorgung auf, da die antiken Aquädukte mit der Zeit zerstört wurden, so daß die städtische Bevölkerung in verstärktem Maße fortzog. Die Vatikanbasilika befand sich dagegen auf der anderen Seite des Flusses und damit außerhalb des antiken Stadtkerns. Sehr bald jedoch bildete sich um die Kirche eine Zitadelle, der sogenannte Borgo, der im 9. Jahrhundert mit Mauern umgeben wurde und zu dem man ausschließlich über den antiken Pons Aelius, die heutige Engelsbrücke, Zugang hatte. Da das Castel Sant'Angelo, die Grabstätte der Kaiserfamilie, die Hadrian im 2. Jahrhundert errichten ließ und die schon im 4. Jahrhundert in eine uneinnehmbare Festung umgebaut wurde, zum päpstlichen Besitz gehörte, konnte der Borgo von hier aus leicht kontrolliert werden. Die Vormachtstellung von St. Peter gegenüber der Lateranbasilika wurde schließlich im frühen 13. Jahrhundert besiegelt, als neben der Kirche ein Palast erbaut wurde, der seit dem 15. Jahrhundert nach Erweiterungsarbeiten als eigentlicher Sitz des Papstes diente.

Die Entscheidung von Papst Julius II. (1503–1513) zu Beginn seiner Amtszeit, die jahrtausendalte Kirche Kon-

time had been reduced to the point that it was insufficient to carry out the pontifical ceremonies that the court and the pope's role as sovereign were making more and more complex. Nicholas V, the first pontiff to make Rome his permanent residence after exile in Avignon and the Schism of the West, had planned to modernize the basilica; he had even started to construct a new tribune after Bernardo Rossellino's design, which extended well beyond the Early Christian apse. The plan provided for the maintenance of the early longitudinal body; the reinforcement of the external side aisles, which opened onto new chapels with the same format; the construction of a great dome – perhaps without a drum – at the crossing of the five ancient naves and a new, wider transept, and – as stated above – the construction, which was to extend far beyond the old apse, of a deep tribune where pontifical functions would be carried out. Perhaps convinced by Leon Battista Alberti, who must have thought the idea too limited, or perhaps too Florentine, Nicholas V soon had work stopped, when the wall of the new apse, seven meters wide, had reached less than two meters in height. But, to be sure, the idea of "renovating" the old basilica according to new Tuscan models (there would have been a clear derivation from Brunelleschian churches, San Lorenzo in particular, since it had been conceived of as an evocation of Early Christian basilicas) constituted, together with the simultaneous decision to have Beato Angelico decorate the new chapel of the Vatican palace, appropriately named the Niccolina, the clearest case of a pontiff taking a position with respect to contemporary culture.

First of all, in Florence, and then immediately afterwards in the most advanced centers in Italy and Europe, that cultural revolution we call – and which defined itself as such – by the name of Humanism was underway in the early years of the Quattrocento. Starting with a new conception of man, it challenged the roots of the previous culture. With the invention of History (in the broad sense of *invenire*, to discover) it gave a new sense of how time passes; with the discovery of perspective, it made space rationally measurable; with the theory of proportions, another re-discovery from antiquity, it made the human figure the measure of all things. By going against the structure of the culture which had been handed down to them, the humanists had gone so far as to doubt the authority of the Church, or religious culture, at least. By basing their findings on the historical knowledge of the Latin language, Lorenzo Valla (1405–1457) and Nicholas Cusano (1401–1464) demonstrated that the so-called Donation of Constantine, the document on which the Church of Rome had founded the claims to its temporal dominion, was a forgery dating to much later than the fourth century. By appealing to classical antiquity, Coluccio Salutati and Leonardo Bruni placed non-religious – or values clearly stated as secular – at the base of political ethics.

The project of Nicholas V for St. Peter's, entrusted to one of the leading figures of the Florentine humanistic revolution, essentially consisted in emending the ancient

stantins niederzureißen und eine von Grund auf neue, programmatisch moderne Peterskirche zu errichten, läßt sich nicht allein durch ästhetische Erwägungen erklären, da mit der alten Basilika eine große historische, ideologische und religiöse Bedeutung verknüpft war. Sicherlich wies das Mittelschiff unübersehbare statische Probleme auf. Ebenso hatte die unregelmäßige Aufeinanderfolge von Kapellen, Oratorien, Altären und Grabdenkmälern die ursprüngliche Schlichtheit der Struktur beeinträchtigt und erschien als eine zufällige Anordnung. Auch die Apsis mit ihren verminderten Ausmaßen zeigte sich mittlerweile für die Feier der päpstlichen Zeremonien, die der Hofstaat und die Herrscherrolle des Papstes zunehmend komplizierter gestalteten, als unzureichend. Schon Nikolaus V., der als erster Papst nach dem Exil in Avignon und dem Schisma des Westens dauerhaft in Rom residierte, hatte eine Modernisierung der Basilika geplant und bereits mit dem Bau einer neuen Tribuna begonnen, die auf Entwürfen Bernardo Rossellinos beruhte und weit hinter der frühchristlichen Apsis lag. Der Entwurf sah die Erhaltung des ursprünglichen Längsbaus vor und eine Verstärkung der äußeren Seitenschiffe, die längs der neuen, regelmäßigen Kapellen entstehen sollten. Außerdem war der Bau einer großen Kuppel – möglicherweise ohne Tambour – am Kreuzungspunkt der fünf alten Schiffe mit dem neuen, erweiterten Querschiff geplant und, wie erwähnt, die Errichtung einer tiefen Tribuna weit hinter der alten Apsis, in der die päpstlichen Zeremonien stattfinden sollten. Vielleicht von Leon Battista Alberti überzeugt, der das zu begrenzte bzw. zu florentinische Vorhaben beurteilen sollte, ließ Nikolaus V. schon bald die Arbeiten unterbrechen, als die 7 m breite Mauer der neuen Apsis eine

Cross section of the ancient basilica, in M. Ferrabosco, *Architettura della Basilica di San Pietro in Vaticano*, second edition, Rome 1684, tav. 5

Querschnitt der alten Basilika, aus: M. Ferrabosco, *Architettura della Basilica di San Pietro in Vaticano*, 2. Auflage, Rom 1684, Tafel 5

text by correcting its errors, but leaving the scheme intact. Like an ancient manuscript, the philological method reconstructed the authentic text on the one hand, while on the other – rather, precisely for this reason – it established its value. It was a position of courageous progressivism – Nicholas V had himself been a humanist – but it was one which tended to place the new culture within the context of the Church, rather than to make Humanism one of the pilasters of the church after the Great Schism and the Council of Constance, which had risked undermining the primacy of the pontiff. For this same reason, Nicholas V summoned Beato Angelico, the learned Dominican painter who had located the perspectival revolution within Thomist culture, identifying Brunelleschian space with divine light. Leon Battista Alberti – the most coherent and lucid of the humanists – could not help pointing out the limits in Bernardo Rossellino's plan: in the treatise *De re aedificatoria*, presented to Nicholas V himself in 1452, he explained the intellectual nature of architecture, which was understood as the definition of the ideational more than the constructive process. It is thus no surprise that he used all his influence on the pope, and then on his successors, to stop an operation which must have seemed very limited and not worthy of the Vatican basilica.

The cultural horizons of Julius II were completely different from those of Nicholas V. This is evident from the choice of the architect to whom he entrusted the very prestigious task of the new St. Peter's, as well as the enlargement of the Vatican palace with the grandiose Belvedere courtyard – projects which are not only chronologically connected. From the position of cardinal, Giuliano Della Rovere, nephew of Sixtus IV (1471–1484), was not only the privileged patron, but also a friend of Giuliano da Sangallo, the great Florentine architect who was more than any other the spiritual heir of Brunelleschi. It was not simply that the future pontiff commissioned him for the palace he was to have built in Savona in 1494, after the flight from Rome; they were also together for two long years in France. Yet, as soon as he was elected pontiff in October of 1503, Julius II entrusted his grandiose projects to Donato Bramante, an architect who was unknown to him up to that time and with whom he certainly was not on familiar terms, like he was with Sangallo. Moreover, in Rome, he had only built the cloisters of Santa Maria della Pace up to that time (begun in 1500 and finished in 1504), and perhaps the Tempietto in San Pietro in Montorio, if the date of 1502 as recorded in an inscription in the crypt of the sacellum is correct. Such an unusual – and of necessity important – choice must have been dictated by a "good" reason, all the more so, since both before and after his rise to the throne, Julius II always proved to be sensible, lucid, and competent in his artistic and cultural choices. Evidently, if the Della Rovere pope turned down a famous architect he had a great deal of esteem for and with whom he had been friends for ten years in favor of another who was unknown to him, he must have understood, first of all,

Höhe von weniger als 2 m erreicht hatte. Doch sein Vorhaben, die alte Basilika nach den neuen toskanischen Vorbildern zu „erneuern"– deutlich wäre dabei der Einfluß der Kirchen Brunelleschis gewesen, insbesondere von San Lorenzo, die als Evokation der antiken frühchristlichen Kirchen aufgefaßt wurde –, sowie der gleichzeitige Beschluß, die neue Kapelle des Vatikanpalastes von Beato Angelico ausstatten zu lassen, die deshalb den Namen Cappella Niccolina trug, waren sicherlich die klarste Stellungnahme des Papstes gegenüber der zeitgenössischen Kultur.

Seit dem frühen 15. Jahrhundert hatte sich vor allem in Florenz, aber bald darauf auch in den fortschrittlichsten Städten Italiens und Europas, jene Kulturrevolution herausgebildet, die wir – so definiert sie sich auch selbst – als Humanismus bezeichnen. Von einer neuen Auffassung des Menschen ausgehend, hatte sie die Wurzeln der vorausgegangenen Kultur in Frage gestellt. Mit der Erfindung der Geschichte (im Sinne des lateinischen Wortes „invenire", wiederfinden) hatte der Humanismus der Zeit einen neuen Sinn gegeben; mit der Entdeckung der Perspektive hatte er den Raum rational meßbar gemacht; mit der Theorie der Proportionen, ebenfalls eine Wiederentdeckung der Antike, hatte er den Menschen als allgemeingültiges Maß festgelegt. Die Humanisten waren durch die Ablehnung der ihnen überlieferten Kultur nicht weit davon entfernt, auch die Autorität der Kirche oder zumindest die religiöse kulturelle Tradition in Frage zu stellen. Mit Hilfe der historischen Kenntnis der lateinischen Sprache hatten Lorenzo Valla (1404–1457) und Nikolaus von Kues (1401–1464) gezeigt, daß das Dokument der sogenannten Konstantinischen Schenkung, auf die die römische Kirche die Voraussetzungen ihrer weltlichen Herrschaft gegründet hatte, eine Fälschung und sehr viel später nach dem 4. Jahrhundert zu datieren war. Mit ihrer Hinwendung zum klassischen Altertum hatten Coluccio Salutati und Leonardo Bruni der politischen Ethik nichtreligiöse bzw. ganz eindeutig weltliche Werte zugrunde gelegt.

Das Vorhaben Nikolaus' V. für St. Peter wurde einem der Nebenakteure der florentinischen humanistischen Revolution übertragen und bestand im wesentlichen in der Berichtigung des antiken Textes, wobei die Fehler verbessert werden, das Grundschema jedoch unverändert bleiben sollten. Wie bei einer antiken Handschrift stellt die philologische Methode einerseits den authentischen Text wieder her, auf der anderen Seite – und das gerade deswegen – entscheidet sie über seinen Wert. Diese Haltung Nikolaus' V., der selbst ein Humanist war, zeugte von einem mutigen Fortschrittsdenken, das allerdings die neue Kultur in die Kirche einpassen und den Humanismus nach dem Großen Schisma und dem Konzil von Konstanz, die die Vorrangstellung des Papstes bedroht hatten, zu einer Säule der Kirche machen sollte. Eben aus diesem Grund berief Nikolaus V. den Maler Beato Angelico, einen gebildeten Dominikaner, der die perspektivische Revolution in die thomistische Kultur eingeordnet hatte, indem er den Raum Brunelleschis mit dem göttlichen Licht gleichsetzte. Die Begrenztheit des Entwurfs Bernardo Rossellinos mußte

that, as pontiff, he would have to make decisions different from those he had made as cardinal, and he must have understood that Bramante's way of creating architecture was much more consonant with his policy than that of Sangallo. Thus, we must look for the reasons for his intense building activity and for the choice of Bramante in Julius II's plan for the pontificate.

Raised by Sixtus IV to the purple at a very young age, Giuliano Della Rovere seemed to be destined to the tiara ever since the period of Sixtus' pontificate. When he was elected pontiff, he was almost sixty, and had spent the last decade of his life in exile, having been sent away from Rome because of his firm opposition to Alexander VI Borgia (1492–1503). Being far away from Rome when he was no longer young did not, however, seem to have quashed his ambition. Rather, it contributed to his lucid understanding of the overall political panorama of Europe, in the very period in which the conflicts between the great nations were being defined. The entire century was characterized by such conflicts, which were touched off by the struggle for domination in Italy. As a counter-proposal to the monarchies on the other side of the Alps and to their modern way of organization, Julius II suggested the idea of a dominant role for the pontiff of Rome, who was both the spiritual head of Christianity and the political sovereign on whom Italian – and hence European – balances were centered. At first he made an alliance in the League of Cambrai (1508) with France and the Empire against Venice, only to turn the allies against France (1511) in the Holy League.

The question of the "new St. Peter's" is hence linked, and this time in absolutely explicit terms, to the claim of the role of the pontiff as the successor to the prince of the Apostles. But, unlike Nicholas V, Julius II did not have the problem of a learned philological revival of the ancient scheme of the basilica that would mark the reconciliation of Christianity and Humanism, as in the early years of the Cinquecento. Modern culture was no longer to be integrated into a tradition: it had to be used to give a visible representation to the primate of the Church. It is for this reason that, in an ever more refined formal search, Julius II realized he needed not the scholarly Giuliano da Sangallo, heir to the Florentine figurative tradition that had been evolving in the second half of the Quattrocento – think of Botticelli, Pollaiolo or Piero di Cosimo – but the grandiloquent Bramante, the architect who was previously educated at Urbino, where Piero della Francesca (in order to reconcile the Florentine and humanistic concept of *historia* and biconvex vision, worked out in detail by the Flemish) had worked out his idea of form as universal representation, significant in itself. He later compared and expanded his Pierfrancescan education in Milan with the more perceptive heir of Florentine Neoplatonism, Leonardo da Vinci, with whom Bramante was friend and colleague. The new St. Peter's designed by Bramante was conceived of as a visible representation of the pontifical authority which finds the reasons for its primacy

Leon Battista Alberti, dem konsequentesten Humanisten, notgedrungen auffallen: In seinem Traktat „De re aedificatoria", den er Nikolaus V. 1452 vorgestellt hatte, hatte er den intellektuellen Charakter der Baukunst dargelegt, die eher als Vollendung eines ideellen als eines konstruktiven Prozesses verstanden werden sollte. Es ist daher nicht verwunderlich, daß er seinen ganzen Einfluß auf den Papst und später auch auf dessen Nachfolger ausübte, um ein Vorhaben zu verhindern, das ihm äußerst eingeschränkt und der Vatikanbasilika unwürdig erscheinen mußte.

Der kulturelle Horizont Julius' II. war dagegen vollkommen anders gelagert. Dies läßt schon die Wahl des Architekten erkennen, dem er den äußerst prestigeträchtigen Auftrag für die neue Peterskirche sowie die nicht nur zeitlich daran anknüpfende Erweiterung des Vatikanpalastes durch den großartigen Belvedere-Hof anvertraute. Als Kardinal war Giuliano Della Rovere, der Neffe Sixtus' IV. (1471–1484), nicht nur ein bevorzugter Auftraggeber Giulianos da Sangallo gewesen, sondern vielleicht sogar ein Freund des bedeutenden florentinischen Architekten, der mehr als jeder andere als geistiger Erbe Brunelleschis galt. Der zukünftige Papst hatte ihn nicht nur nach seiner Flucht aus Rom im Jahr 1494 mit der Errichtung seines Palastes in Savona beauftragt, sondern die beiden hatten zwei Jahre gemeinsam in Frankreich verbracht. Und dennoch wandte sich Julius II. unmittelbar nach seiner Wahl zum Papst im Oktober 1503 für seine ehrgeizigen Pläne an den Architekten Donato Bramante, der ihm bis dahin nicht bekannt war und mit dem er sicherlich keinen Umgang pflegte, wie mit Sangallo. Hinzu kam, daß Bramante zu jenem Zeitpunkt in Rom nur den Kreuzgang von Santa Maria della Pace, der 1500 begonnen und 1504 vollendet wurde, und möglicherweise auch den Tempietto in San Pietro in Montorio erbaut hatte, wenn das Datum 1502 auf der Inschrift in der Gedächtniskrypta verläßlich ist. Hinter dieser ungewöhnlichen und daher signifikanten Wahl muß sich ein „mächtiger" Grund verbergen, umso mehr, als Julius II. sich sowohl vor als auch nach seiner Wahl zum Papst bei seinen künstlerischen und kulturellen Entscheidungen stets einsichtig, vernünftig und fachkundig gezeigt hatte. Wenn der Papst auf einen berühmten Architekten, den er schätzte und mit dem ihn eine zehnjährige Freundschaft verband, zugunsten eines anderen, ihm Unbekannten verzichtete, hatte er in erster Linie offensichtlich begriffen, daß er als Papst andere Entscheidungen treffen mußte als zu seiner Kardinalszeit. Zudem muß er verstanden haben, daß die Baukunst Bramantes sehr viel mehr mit seiner Politik harmonierte als diejenige Sangallos. Deshalb sind die Gründe seiner überaus intensiven Bautätigkeit und der Wahl Bramantes im Pontifikatsprogramm Julius' II. zu suchen.

Von Sixtus IV. noch sehr jung zum Kardinal ernannt, schien Giuliano Della Rovere schon für die sixtinische Amtszeit für die Tiara bestimmt. Als er zum Papst gewählt wurde, war er indes schon beinahe 60 Jahre alt. Die letzten zehn Jahre seines Lebens verbrachte er im Exil, da er wegen seiner standhaften Opposition gegen Alexander VI. aus

Maerten van Heemskerck, view of the old longitudinal building in the area of the dome and the choir.
Berlin, Staatliche Museen Preussischer Kulturbesitz, Kupferstichkabinett, Berliner Skizzenbuch, II, f. 52r

Maerten van Heemskerck, Ansicht des alten Longitudinalbaus im Bereich der Kuppel und des Chores.
Berlin, Staatliche Museen Preussischer Kulturbesitz, Kupferstichkabinett, Berliner Skizzenbuch, II, Folio 52r

in history. The basilica imagined by Julius II and conceived of by Bramante would be defined much later by Michelangelo (who also clashed with the architect) as "chiara e schietta, luminosa e isolata a torno" (clear and pure, luminous and isolated on all sides). This is exactly the same logic of light and space in the frescoes of those same years and for the same pontiff which Raphael was painting in the Vatican palace. Like Bramante, Raphael was also from Urbino, and took Piero della Francesca as a point of departure in order to compare himself with contemporary Florentine culture. Perhaps he was even summoned to Rome by Bramante himself. Like Imperial architecture, the new St. Peter's was to have the same expansive breadth, the same formal perfection, the same linguistical refinement. When the sources mention the Bramantesque desire to put the dome of the Pantheon on the basilica of Maxentius in the new St. Peter's, they are doing nothing other than re-stating the intention to erect a Christian temple on the same par as, if not superior to, the grandiosity of the ancients. The new St. Peter's was hence thought of as a *monumentum*, and as such, in its very form, showed the historical roots of the authority of the Church, the identity of faith and reason. Thus the physical remains of the ancient basilica could be sacrificed, because the roots of the way of designing the edifice were historical, and could rival the ancients if not surpass them in magnificence.

The projected *iter* taken by Bramante and the pontiff is complex and much debated by the critics. The reconstruction of successive ideas is linked to hypotheses of the temporal distribution of the drawings which have survived, in any event, in a number always far inferior to the "infinite" ones mentioned by Vasari. They must have been drafted in the two years between the election of Julius II, in the winter of 1503–1504, and the beginning of 1506 (in fact, the cornerstone was laid, evidently according to a defined project, on 18 April, 1506). The different historical reconstructions based on still extant drawings and on documents previous to the beginning of the construction put forward different hypotheses on the articulation of the plan and on the chronological succession of the projects. Without entering into these discussions (which would lead too far astray from our subject), it should in any event be noted that all recent studies stress the dialectic which must have cropped up between the architect and his patron, as is borne out by the complexity of the questions concerning the construction of the new temple, which were raised both before the most advanced architectural culture of the time – which in the planning was experimenting on itself, its methods and its languages – as well as the ambition of the pope, who was explicitly presenting himself as the "new Solomon", the Biblical constructor of the temple of Jerusalem and, as *pontifex maximus*, successor of the Roman emperors. It was almost certainly Bramante who wanted to adopt the *quincunx* scheme, or a plan with central symmetry with respect to a cross (with a central dome and four minor lateral ones). This type of plan char-

dem Hause Borgia (1492–1503) Rom verlassen hatte. Die Entfernung von Rom und sein Alter konnten dennoch seinen Ehrgeiz nicht dämpfen; im Gegenteil, sie hatten dazu beigetragen, ihn das komplizierte politische Panorama Europas klar erkennen zu lassen, in dem sich in jenen Jahren die Konflikte zwischen den großen Nationalstaaten abzeichneten, die das gesamte Jahrhundert prägen sollten und mit dem Kampf um die Vorherrschaft in Italien begannen. Den Monarchien jenseits der Alpen und ihrer modernen Organisation stellte Julius II. die Idee der vorherrschenden Rolle des römischen Papstes entgegen, gleichzeitig spirituelles Oberhaupt der Christenheit und politischer Herrscher, um den sich die italienischen und damit auch die europäischen Mächte anordnen sollten. Zunächst verbündete er sich in der Liga von Cambrai (1508) mit Frankreich und dem Deutschen Reich gegen Venedig, später aber (1511) ging er mit der Heiligen Liga ein Bündnis gegen Frankreich ein.

Das Problem der „neuen Peterskirche" war also – und diesmal sehr ausdrücklich – mit dem Anspruch der päpstlichen Rolle als Nachfolger des Apostelfürsten verbunden. Im Unterschied zu Nikolaus V. stellte sich Julius II. jedoch nicht die Frage nach einer gelehrten philologischen Wiederherstellung des alten Basilikaschemas, das die Aussöhnung von Christentum und Humanismus zum Ausdruck brachte, die bereits im frühen 16. Jahrhundert zustande gekommen war. Die moderne Kultur sollte nun nicht mehr in eine Tradition integriert werden, sondern als sichtbare Darstellung des kirchlichen Primats dienen. Aus diesem Grund griff Julius II. nicht auf den gelehrten Giuliano da Sangallo zurück, den Erben der figurativen florentinischen Tradition, die sich in der zweiten Hälfte des 15. Jahrhunderts mit ihrer formalen, immer anspruchsvolleren Suche weiterentwickelt hatte – man denke nur an Botticelli, Pollaiolo oder Piero di Cosimo; vielmehr wählte er den würdevollen Architekten Bramante, der zunächst in Urbino ausgebildet wurde. Dort hatte Piero della Francesca an der an sich schon bedeutsamen Idee der Form als universaler Darstellung gearbeitet, um die florentinische und humanistische Geschichtsauffassung und die detailbezogenen Vorstellungen der flämischen Künstler miteinander in Einklang zu bringen. Danach setzte er seine durch Piero della Francesca geprägte Ausbildung in Mailand fort, wo ihm mit Leonardo da Vinci der scharfsinnigste Erbe des florentinischen Neuplatonismus gegenüberstand, ein Freund und Arbeitskollege Bramantes. Der Entwurf Bramantes für die neue Peterskirche war als eine sichtbare Darstellung der päpstlichen Autorität konzipiert, die die Grundlagen ihrer Vormachtstellung aus der Geschichte ableitete. Die Basilika, wie sie sich Julius II. vorgestellt und Bramante entworfen hatte, wurde später von Michelangelo „hell und ebenmäßig, lichtvoll und freistehend" verwirklicht, obwohl dieser sich mit dem Architekten kritisch auseinandersetzen mußte. Diese logische Identität von Licht und Raum ist auch bei den Fresken zu erkennen, die Raffael – ebenfalls ein Maler aus Urbino, der auch von Piero della Francesca ausgegangen war, um sich mit der zeitgenössischen florentinischen Kultur auseinanderzusetzen – in denselben Jahren und für

acterizes the most famous of the projects studied before the beginning of the construction, the one laid out on sheet A1 in the Uffizi, the so-called parchment plan. But it was probably Julius II who would not give up the use of the wall already built by Nicholas V. He refused to consider the idea of moving the tomb of St. Peter, and insisted on the combination of a central scheme with a longitudinal plan. However, apart from the much debated history of the projects, it is certain that immediately after February 1505, Julius II had imagined locating it in the new choir of St. Peter's, transforming it into his own personal chapel (thus called the cappella Julia), or tomb. He had Michelangelo summoned from Florence to Rome in order to sculpt it, and after having drawn up the contract, in March of the same year, Michelangelo went to Carrara for eight months to choose the marble necessary for the pontifical sepulchre. In January of 1506, he went back to Rome to get started on the work. On 17 April, 1506, however, right on the eve of the placement of the first stone of the new basilica, the sculptor fled Rome, blaming the failure of his project on Bramante, with schemes which are not altogether clear. Inasmuch as the conflict between the architect from Urbino and the Florentine sculptor can be read – as it was, in fact – as the incompatibility of personalities, it is certain that in the winter of 1506, a crucial step in the conception of the new St. Peter's must have taken place. Having shelved – although without giving up on it – the project for his own monument, probably to concentrate all available funds on the construction, Julius II took a decisive step he could not go back on. With the first two west piers that were to sustain the dome in place in April of 1507, and the consequent destruction of the last bays of the longitudinal body of the medieval basilica, neither he nor his successors could turn back. And by preferring Bramante to Michelangelo, Julius II symbolically decided that the new enterprise should fall under the aegis of architecture, and not of sculpture, and that all the arts would have to subordinate their effects to the determination of space. Furthermore, he established the fact that the new construction would be an expression of concepts, and not the celebration of a single pontiff.

In proposing ideas to the pontiff, in discussing architectural solutions within its own confines, in organizing a construction yard that could only be thought of as longterm, the architectural culture of the early Cinquecento was forced to reformulate the methods, tools and goals of its way of working. The philological research of the past twenty years has carefully analyzed the massive graphic documentation still housed in the Gabinetto Disegni e Stampe at the Uffizi in Florence, including sheets once in the possession of Antonio da Sangallo the Younger (and for more than a quarter of a century at that, from 1520 to 1546), the architect of the construction of St. Peter's, in the guise of heir and collector of the drawings left by his predecessors. The drawing cited above with the inventory number of one of the Florentine collections on architecture (Uffizi 1 Architettura, or, in abbreviated

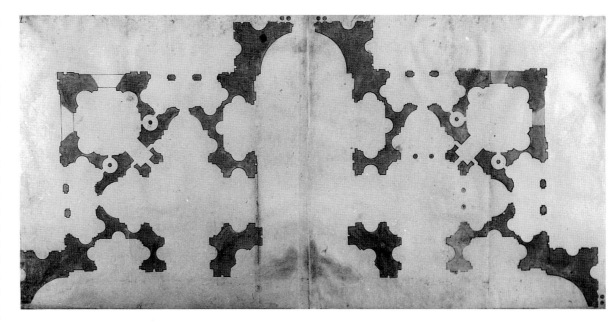

denselben Papst im Vatikanpalast anfertigte; möglicherweise war er sogar von Bramante nach Rom berufen worden. Die neue Peterskirche besaß die gleiche Weiträumigkeit, formale Auserlesenheit und sprachliche Feinheit wie die Architektur der Kaiserzeit. Wenn die zeitgenössischen Quellen auf das Vorhaben Bramantes hinweisen, in der neuen Basilika die Kuppel des Pantheon auf die Maxentiusbasilika zu setzen, unterstreichen sie damit die Absicht, ein christliches Bauwerk zu schaffen, das der Größe der antiken nicht nur gleichkommt, sondern sie sogar überragt. Die neue Peterskirche war demnach als Denkmal gedacht, das mit seiner monumentalen Gestalt die historischen Wurzeln der kirchlichen Autorität, der Einheit von Glauben und Vernunft ausdrücken sollte. Die Überreste der alten Basilika konnten geopfert werden, da die Planungsweise des Baus durch historische Gründe bestimmt wurde und er somit mit der Antike konkurrieren und sogar anstreben konnte, ihre Großartigkeit zu übertreffen.

Der von Bramante und dem Papst unternommene Planungsprozeß ist komplex und in der Kunstgeschichte umstritten. Die Rekonstruktion der nachfolgenden Ideen ist mit der Hypothese einer Chronologie der verbliebenen Zeichnungen verbunden, deren Zahl sich allerdings weit unter der von Vasari angegebenen „unendlichen Anzahl" bewegt. Sie dürften in den beiden Jahren zwischen der Wahl Julius' II. im Winter 1503/1504 und Anfang 1506 angefertigt worden sein; denn der Grundstein wurde aufgrund eines offensichtlich endgültigen Entwurfs am 18. April 1506 gelegt. Die unterschiedlichen historischen Rekonstruktionen beruhen auf noch heute erhaltenen Zeichnungen und Dokumenten, die aus der Zeit vor dem Baubeginn stammen; sie legen verschiedene Hypothesen hinsichtlich der Entwicklung der Baupläne und der chronologischen Reihenfolge der Entwürfe dar. Ohne auf diese Debatten näher einzugehen, was zu weit vom Thema wegführen würde, soll jedoch darauf hingewiesen werden, daß alle neueren Forschungen die Dialektik betonen, die

Donato Bramante, presentation drawing of the project for St. Peter's. Florence, Uffizi, Gabinetto Disegni e Stampe, 1A

Donato Bramante, Präsentationszeichnung zum Projekt der Peterskirche. Florenz, Uffizien, Gabinetto Disegni e Stampe, 1A

form, UA1) is a large sheet of parchment longer than one meter, wider than fifty centimeters, and precisely – since drawings are usually measured in millimeters – 1110 x 540 mm. The original project must have had even greater dimensions, since the parchment seems to have been cut on all four sides. The accuracy with which the lines were first traced in brown ink and then gone over with light ochre watercolor, the fact that the materials were precious (not the usual paper, but costly parchment), the large format of the plan, on a scale of 1:150, are all elements which have led critics to maintain – and for once unanimously – that UA1 was among the drawings presented to Julius II by Bramante: this means that the pontiff was capable – apart from esthetically appreciating the drawing – of deciphering the formal abstraction of a plan. From the scale drawing, he could understand it in depth and evaluate the architect (something which was not at all common in the period). Moreover, the object under discussion between the pontiff and his architect was, from the moment in which the sheet was presented, mainly a planimetric development of the new basilica, that is, to use a term from the period, its *icnografia*. A laconic note by Antonio da Sangallo on the verso identifies it as a plan of St. Peter's by Bramante which was not used ("Pianta di S[an]to Pietro di mano di bramante che non ebbe ef[f]etto") because the quincunx scheme proposed by Bramante, which is evident if the other half of the drawing is completed, did not meet with Julius II's definitive approval: for the plan – which, like almost all the drawings done at this phase, there are no known elevations – there was no model made in wood later to make things clearer, as happened instead when the project was definitively approved in April 1506. UA6 is another presentation drawing, but of a different type. It is a large sheet of paper (918 x 503 mm), accurately done in brown watercolor. It, too, has been cut, but still presents – unlike UA1 – the entire plan of the church, according to a longitudinal scheme ending in a choir surrounded by an ambulatory, which in turn, provides access to deep side chapels. At the ends of the transept there are two towers, while the central axis of the basilica is articulated by five domes having the same width of the two domes in the two arms of the transept. An inscription on the verso, in the hand of Antonio da Sangallo, identifies the sheet with the "Opinione e disegnio Di fraiocondo per santo pietro Di Roma" (idea and drawing of Fra Giocondo for St. Peter's in Rome). This is the name of the then very elderly Fra Giocondo, a learned architect with a profound knowledge of building technology. He, too, got his training at Urbino, but was later active at many courts in Italy and France, where he is still documented in 1505. This would explain the curious presence of elements (like the ambulatory and the radial chapels, or the towers at the sides of the transept) taken from cathedrals on the other side of the Alps, which were, among other things, admired by Julius II. But above all, it is the definition of "opinione" (idea) which explains the nature of the drawing which, since it is so different from the one started by Bramante, could

zwischen dem Architekten und seinem Auftraggeber entstanden war. Dies bezeugt die Komplexität der Fragen hinsichtlich des Baus des neuen Gotteshauses, die sowohl die fortschrittlichere architektonische Kultur betrafen, die in der Planungsphase mit ihren eigenen Methoden und ihrer Ausdrucksweise experimentierte, als auch den Ehrgeiz des Papstes, der ausdrücklich als „neuer Salomon" auftrat, der biblische Erbauer des Tempels von Jerusalem, und sich in seiner Funktion des Pontifex Maximus als Nachfolger der römischen Kaiser verstand. Höchstwahrscheinlich wollte Bramante das Zentralbauschema anwenden, das eine Zentralsymmetrie zu einem Kreuz mit einer Hauptkuppel und vier kleineren Nebenkuppeln vorsah. Dieses Projekt kennzeichnet den bekanntesten Entwurf der vor Baubeginn studierten Pläne, das Blatt A1, den sogenannten Pergamentplan, der in den Uffizien aufbewahrt wird. Wahrscheinlich aber wollte Julius II. nicht auf die bereits von Nikolaus V. errichtete Mauer verzichten, lehnte eine mögliche Verlegung des Petrusgrabes ab und bestand auf der Kombination von Zentral- und Longitudinalbau. Unabhängig von der vieldiskutierten Geschichte der Entwürfe steht jedoch fest, daß Julius II. unmittelbar nach Februar 1505 im neuen Chor von St. Peter, der in seine persönliche Kapelle umgewandelt werden und daher Cappella Julia heißen sollte, sein eigenes Grabmal aufstellen lassen wollte. Dazu hatte er Michelangelo von Florenz nach Rom geholt, der nach dem Vertragsabschluß im März für acht Monate nach Carrara zog, um die Marmorblöcke für das Papstgrab auszuwählen. Im Januar 1506 kehrte er nach Rom zurück und begann mit der Arbeit. Am 17. April 1506, einen Tag vor der Grundsteinlegung der neuen Basilika, floh der Bildhauer aus Rom, wobei er Bramante beschuldigte, seinen Plan durch unsaubere Machenschaften zum Scheitern gebracht zu haben. Auch wenn die Auseinandersetzung zwischen dem Architekten aus Urbino und dem florentinischen Bildhauer mit der Unvereinbarkeit ihrer Charaktere erklärt werden kann – was auch so geschah –, muß im Winter 1506 eine kritische Phase der Konzeption der neuen Peterskirche eingetreten sein. Julius II. hatte das Projekt für sein persönliches Denkmal aufgeschoben, ohne jedoch darauf zu verzichten, da er wahrscheinlich alle verfügbaren Geldmittel in den Kirchenbau einfließen lassen wollte, und er hatte damit einen entscheidenden und unwiderruflichen Schritt getan. Nach der Aufstellung der ersten beiden Westpfeiler, die die Kuppel stützen, im April 1507 und nach dem Abriß der letzten Joche des Longitudinalbaus der mittelalterlichen Basilika konnten weder er noch seine Nachfolger zurück. Julius II. entschied durch die Wahl Bramantes zuungunsten Michelangelos auf symbolische Weise, daß das neue Bauwerk von der Architektur und nicht von der Skulptur geprägt werden sollte und daß alle Künste ihre Wirkungskraft dem Raum unterzuordnen hätten. Außerdem legte er fest, daß das neue Bauwerk Ausdruck von Ideen sein und nicht der Verherrlichung eines einzelnen Papstes dienen sollte.

Bei den Vorschlägen ihrer Ideen gegenüber dem Papst, bei der Diskussion über architektonische Lösungen in den

not have been made before 1514/1515, the years when Leo X put the most competent expert of the era next to the young, inexpert Raphael as Bramante's successor. In a letter of 1507, in fact, Fra Giocondo mentions that he preferred the offer by the Republic of Venice to the requests of Paris, even though he had been requested by the Pope ("essendo richiesto dal papa"). Since the architect was in the service of Venice at the beginning of 1506, Julius II evidently consulted the elderly monk even before construction was underway, asking him for an "opinion", a general idea of which seems to be given in sheet UA6, which uses absolutely incredible dimensions (Frommel has calculated that in order to make room for such a basilica, it would have been necessary to demolish half of the pontifical palace and the Sixtine Chapel). It was not a true project related to a specific place, then, but only an idea from which to draw inspiration for plans for the new St. Peter's.

But the comparison of the ideas of the different architects did not always happen at a distance. The recto of another drawing in the Uffizi, UA8, shows a variant of the large parchment plan. It is a sheet of paper, not as large as the two previous ones (410 x 397 mm), and shows, carefully traced in ink, a *quincunx* scheme. However, it is different from Bramante's project in its considerable reinforcement of the supporting structure and in its accentuated hierarchical subordination of the lateral to the central areas. This is not a preliminary idea, but a real, studied, carefully meditated project, and this is clear from the scale in Roman spans traced in in the lower part, and from the writing in the hand of Giuliano da Sangallo. Although Julius II had commissioned Bramante for the project, in 1504, in fact, he called his old architect to the court in Rome, and apparently, without giving him an official role, showed him the more elaborate ideas of his more clever colleague. The drawing on the recto of UA8 thus represents Sangallo's criticism of Bramante's UA1. It is an accusation of insufficient technical competence: the reinforcement of the piers – which really are too slender in the parchment plan – implies a controversy concerning the static order, even if Giuliano's Florentine training hindered his understanding, or ability to appreciate, the grandiosity implicit in the fluid passage from larger to smaller spaces conceived by Bramante, or the coordinated, progressive, grandiloquent growth of the basilica. Turning the sheet over, however, there is a response from Bramante to the counter-proposal of Sangallo. In sanguine, with rapidly drawn-in strokes, perhaps tracing over the general scheme of his rival with the light behind it, Bramante answered Giuliano da Sangallo *per figuram*, accepting his criticism of the static order, as long as it took the enlargement of the pilasters into account, but criticizing in his turn the monotony of the Florentine. In fact, he cleverly introduced, in the lateral spaces, the idea of ambulatories which would have created a hierarchy of space more imaginatively, by distinguishing the space dominated by the main dome from the smaller ones. Above, sketched in rapidly, is the plan of San Lorenzo

eigenen Reihen sowie bei der Organisation einer Bauhütte, die auf lange Sicht geplant werden mußte, war die architektonische Kultur des frühen 16. Jahrhunderts gezwungen, ihre eigenen Methoden, Mittel und Zielsetzungen zu überdenken. Die philologische Forschung der letzten 20 Jahre hat aufmerksam die umfangreiche graphische Dokumentation analysiert, die heute noch insbesondere im Gabinetto Disegni e Stampe der Uffizien in Florenz aufbewahrt wird. Dazu gehören die Blätter, die sich im Besitz Antonios da Sangallo d. J. befanden, der länger als ein Vierteljahrhundert (1520–1546) Architekt an der Bauhütte von St. Peter war und in dieser Funktion als Erbe und Sammler der Zeichnungen seiner Vorgänger angesehen werden kann. Bei der erwähnten Zeichnung mit der Inventarnummer 1 der florentinischen Architektursammlung (Uffizi 1 Architettura bzw. abgekürzt UA1) handelt es sich um ein großes Pergament mit einer Höhe von 1110 mm und einer Breite von 540 mm. Der Originalentwurf dürfte noch größere Ausmaße gehabt haben, da das Pergament an allen vier Seiten beschnitten wurde. Die Sorgfalt, mit der zunächst die Linien in brauner Tinte gezogen und danach mit hellockergelben Aquarellfarben übermalt wurden, die Kostbarkeit des Materials (kein gewöhnliches Papier, sondern das teurere Pergament), eben das große Format des Grundrisses mit dem Maßstab 1:150 – dies alles sind Elemente, die die Kunstgeschichte diesmal einstimmig vermuten lassen, daß die UA1 eine der Zeichnungen gewesen sei, die Bramante Julius II. vorgelegt habe. Das bedeutet, daß der Papst nicht nur in der Lage war, die Zeichnung in ästhetischer Hinsicht zu bewerten, sondern die formale Abstraktheit des Grundrisses zu entschlüsseln und anhand der Zeichnung die Architektur vollständig zu verstehen und zu beurteilen, was zu jener Zeit nicht häufig vorkam. Außerdem ging es bei der Diskussion zwischen dem Papst und seinem Architekten in dem Moment, als ihm die Zeichnung vorgelegt wurde, insbesondere um die planimetrische Ausarbeitung bzw. – um einen Begriff aus jener Epoche zu benutzen – um die Ikonographie der neuen Basilika. Eine lakonische Anmerkung Antonios da Sangallo auf der Rückseite des Blattes verweist auf die „Pianta di S[an]to Pietro di mano di bramante che non ebbe ef[f]etto" (Grundriß von St. Peter aus der Hand Bramantes, der keine Wirkung hatte), weil das von Bramante vorgeschlagene Zentralbauprojekt, das durch die spiegelbildliche Vervollständigung der Zeichnung deutlich wird, nicht die endgültige Zustimmung Julius' II. fand. Dem Grundriß, zu dem – wie bei fast allen in dieser Phase angefertigten Zeichnungen – keine Aufrisse bekannt sind, folgte daher auch kein Holzmodell für weitere Erläuterungen, das allerdings im April 1506 für den endgültig angenommenen Entwurf angefertigt wurde.

Eine weitere Präsentationszeichnung, wenn auch anderer Art, ist die UA6. Der großformatige Papierbogen (918 x 503 mm) ist sorgfältig mit braunen Aquarellfarben bemalt. Auch dieser Bogen ist am Rand beschnitten, zeigt aber im Unterschied zur UA1 den gesamten Grundriß der Kirche. Der Längsbau wird von einem Chor abgeschlossen, um den ein Umgang herumführt, von dem wiederum tiefe Kapellen ausgehen. Am Ende des Quer-

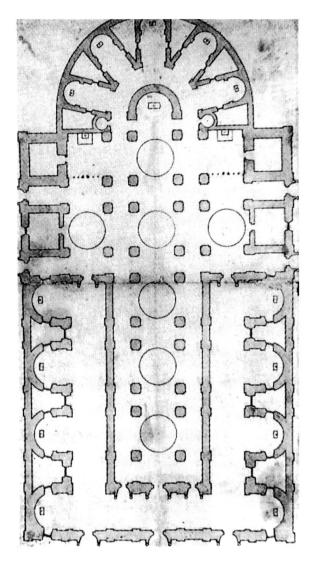

Fra Giocondo, presentation drawing of the project for St. Peter's. Florence, Uffizi, Gabinetto Disegni e Stampe, 6A

Fra Giocondo, Präsentationszeichnung zum Projekt der Peterskirche. Florenz, Uffizien, Gabinetto Disegni e Stampe, 6A

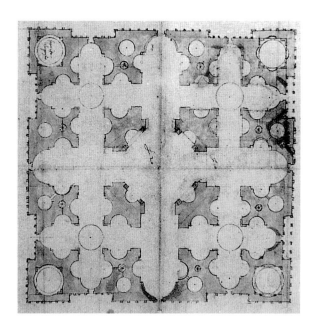

Giuliano da Sangallo, presentation drawing
of the project for St. Peter's.
Florence, Uffizi, Gabinetto Disegni e Stampe, 8Ar

Giuliano da Sangallo, Präsentationszeichnung
zum Projekt der Peterskirche.
Florenz, Uffizien, Gabinetto Disegni e Stampe, 8Ar

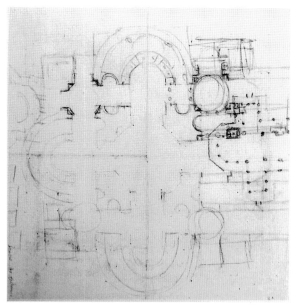

Donato Bramante, plan of the project for St. Peter's.
Florence, Uffizi, Gabinetto Disegni e Stampe, 8Av

Donato Bramante, Grundriß zum Projekt der
Peterskirche.
Florenz, Uffizien, Gabinetto Disegni e Stampe, 8Av

16

in Milano, a late antique building which is exemplary because of its use of ambulatories. It is almost as if, in the lively discussion with the pontiff or the rival architect, he had to justify – with a citation from antiquity – their introduction in the new St. Peter's.

If, up to now, we have only seen the architectural drawing as a means of communication between architects, or between patrons and architects, there is no lack of other sheets drawn in the solitude of concentration necessary for creation. We might define them as internal discussions of the architect with himself. For example, UA20 is a rather large sheet of paper (684 x 470 mm) on which the sanguine marks overlap a thick grid of squared units (each one of which – 3.7 millimeters – corresponding to 5 spans, or 112 centimeters) drawn in ink, evidently prepared so that the architect could have, even though drawing free hand, an immediate comparison in scale. The plan of the old basilica is also drawn in ink, so as to better compare the dimensions of the building that was being imagined with the dimensions of the existing one. During the work, then, the sheet must have proved to be insufficient, because a thin strip of paper has been glued in the left margin. The stroke is altogether different from the elegant, precise hand of the presentation drawings. Rather, in its proceeding with marks which are at times double, it seems to follow the vexation of the architect in his search for a solution. Studied closely, the sheet contains two distinct ideas, or better, the birth of one idea from another. It is enough to observe the four piers destined to support the main dome. The northeast pier is of notably smaller dimensions with respect to the other three, which were evidently drawn in immediately thereafter, as if he wanted to experiment with one, or better (although similar, there are differences), more solutions, by articulating the niches in different ways, enlarging the parastas. In this way, the four squares of the plan show different solutions. Above, rapid, free-hand sketches study the elevation of the inside of the basilica, while, on the verso, marks which are just as rapid

schiffs befinden sich zwei Türme, während die Zentralachse der Basilika durch fünf Kuppeln gegliedert wird, die dieselbe Weite wie die beiden Kuppeln in den Querhausarmen aufweisen. Eine Beschriftung von Antonio da Sangallo auf der Rückseite identifiziert den Bogen mit der „Opinione e disegnio Di fraiocondo per santo pietro Di Roma" (Anschauung und Zeichnung von Fra Giocondo für St. Peter in Rom). Er bezieht sich auf den damals schon hochbetagten Fra Giocondo, einen gebildeten Architekten, der die Techniken der Baukunst gut kannte. Auch er hatte seine Ausbildung in Urbino erhalten, war danach jedoch an zahlreichen Fürstenhöfen in Italien und Frankreich tätig gewesen, wo er noch im Mai 1505 bezeugt ist. Der Name dieses Architekten erklärt einige merkwürdige Elemente – wie beispielsweise den Umgang und den Kapellenkranz oder die seitlichen Türme des Querhauses –, die in den Kathedralen nördlich der Alpen zu finden waren und zudem auch von Julius II. bewundert wurden. Insbesondere erläutert aber der Ausdruck „opinione" (Anschauung) den Charakter der Zeichnung, die aufgrund ihrer so deutlichen Unterschiede zur Arbeit Bramantes nicht aus den Jahren 1514/1515 stammen kann, als Leo X. den sachkundigsten Fachmann jener Zeit dem jungen, unerfahrenen Raffael, der Bramante nachfolgen sollte, zur Seite stellte. In einem Brief von 1507 erwähnt Fra Giocondo, das Angebot der Republik Venedig den Anfragen aus Paris vorgezogen zu haben, obwohl „der Papst nach ihm verlangt" habe. Da der Architekt Anfang 1506 seinen Dienst in Venedig antrat, muß Julius II. den greisen Ordensbruder noch vor Baubeginn mit der Bitte um dessen „Anschauung" um Rat gefragt haben, d. h. um eine grundsätzliche Meinung, denn das Blatt UA6 weist vollkommen unwahrscheinliche Dimensionen auf (Frommel hat errechnet, daß man, um für die geplante Basilika Platz zu schaffen, die Hälfte des Papstpalastes und die Sixtinische Kapelle hätte abreißen müssen). Es handelt sich also hierbei um keinen konkreten Entwurf in bezug auf einen bestimmten Ort, sondern nur um eine Idee, die Anregungen für die Planung der neuen Peterskirche geben sollte.

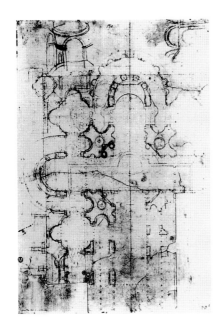

Donato Bramante, drawing of the project for St. Peter's.
Florence, Uffizi, Gabinetto Disegni e Stampe, 20Ar

Donato Bramante, Entwurf zum Projekt der Peterskirche.
Florenz, Uffizien, Gabinetto Disegni e Stampe, 20Ar

fix the ideas for the external elevation and the plan for the dome.

Instead, UA6770 stands almost as a contrary to the sheet for very personal use. It was drawn when construction had already begun; Bramante used it to show the stone-cutters the form of the capitals for the great order to be used on the inside: on a scale of 1:5, he drew, partly in freehand, and partly with a compass and ruler, what we today call an "executive" drawing, or a drawing to give to the workers, limiting himself to drawing only the part that is necessary for a stonecutter to understand.

The architect's need to use the pencil to communicate with his patron, with his workers or, among themselves, to imagine or think about different solutions in a con-struction yard whose dimensions went far beyond any that the Renaissance architect had seen up to that time, forced architectural culture to mould the medium of drawing to meet the new demands – to force its limits, and make it a more malleable dialectic tool. The funda-mental legacy left by these ideas for the new St. Peter's is, if not the profession of architect, at least the use of the drawing as the architect's main tool.

In setting up the organization and financing of the construction yard, Julius II emphasized the dependence of the basilica on the figure of the pontiff. The cathedral – especially the cathedrals in Tuscany or Lombardy – generally had a complex, specific organization, called the *Fabbrica* or *Opera*, in charge of handling problems connected to construction. The different public and ecclesiastical offices of the city were reflected in this organization, and, as the interests of the different social classes were represented there, they often clashed. In the early years of its long history, the construction of the new St. Peter's was different in that it depended strictly on the pontiff and his closed circle. The admin-istration of the Sacro Palazzo, the authority in charge of the pontifical residence, was concerned with the organ-ization of construction, with funds which came from the Camera Apostolica and the Tesoreria Segreta of

Nicht immer jedoch liegt der Vergleich der Ideen unter-schiedlicher Architekten so fern. Die Vorderseite einer weiteren Zeichnung in den Uffizien, der UA8, stellt eine Variante des großen Pergamentplans dar. Der Bogen ist nicht so groß wie die beiden vorherigen (410 x 397 mm); auf ihm ist ein in Tinte angefertigtes und sorgfältig aus-geführtes Zentralbauprojekt zu erkennen, das sich jedoch von Bramantes Entwurf durch die deutliche Verstärkung der Konstruktion und durch die klarere hierarchische Unterordnung der Seitenteile unter den Zentralteil unter-scheidet. Daß es sich hierbei nicht um eine erste Idee, sondern um einen richtigen Bauplan handelt, der ausge-arbeitet und durchdacht war, belegen der Maßstab in römi-schen „Palmi", der unten angegeben ist, sowie einige Be-schriftungen Giulianos da Sangallo. Obwohl Julius II. Bramante mit dem Projekt beauftragt hatte, ließ er 1504 seinen alten Architekten an den römischen Hof berufen und legte ihm, ohne ihm offiziell eine Position anzuver-trauen, offensichtlich die Vorschläge des begabteren Kol-legen vor. Die Zeichnung auf der Vorderseite der UA8 stellt also die Kritik Sangallos an der UA1 Bramantes dar, dem er mangelnde technische Fachkundigkeit vorwarf. Die Verstärkung der Pfeiler, die auf dem Pergamentplan tatsächlich sehr schmal waren, birgt eine Polemik hinsicht-lich der statischen Struktur in sich, auch wenn Giuliano aufgrund seiner florentinischen Ausbildung nicht in der Lage war, die von Bramante ersonnene Großartigkeit der fließenden Übergänge von den größeren zu den kleineren Räumen, die aufeinander abgestimmte, fortschreitende Entwicklung der Basilika zu verstehen und möglicher-weise zu schätzen. Auf der Rückseite des Blattes befindet sich allerdings die Stellungnahme Bramantes zu dem regelrechten Gegenentwurf Sangallos: Die mit einem Rötelstift schnell gezeichneten Linienzüge, die vielleicht im Gegenlicht das Gesamtschema des Rivalen durch-gepaust haben, sind die figurative Antwort Bramantes auf Giuliano da Sangallo. Bramante akzeptiert zwar die Kri-tik in bezug auf die statische Ordnung, da er die Verstär-kung der Pfeiler aufnimmt, kritisiert aber seinerseits die

Donato Bramante and Antonio di Pellegrino, drawing for a capital of the great order on the interior of St. Peter's.
Florence, Uffizi, Gabinetto Disegni e Stampe, 6770Ar

Donato Bramante und Antonio di Pellegrino, Entwurf für das Kapitell der großen inneren Säulen-ordnung in der Peterskirche.
Florenz, Uffizien, Gabinetto Disegni e Stampe, 6770Ar

17

the pope (in reality, the private coffers of the descendent of St. Peter). As a consequence, the architect, Donato Bramante, the bookkeeper (or accountant), Girolamo di Francesco da Siena, the surveyor (the one who checked on the accuracy of the work), Riniero da Pisa, were the same ones who were concerned with the papal construction projects. And those who had control of the substantial funds available for construction – all members of the clergy – were people who were very close to the pontiff and who had his complete trust: Cardinal Fabrizio Santoro, the Archbishop of Taranto Enrico Bruni and, after his death in 1509, Orlando del Carretto and Bartolomeo Ferratini. Even the payments were made by one of the many bankers used by Julius II, Stefano Ghinucci from Siena. Nothing could have been further from the organization of a stable construction yard in any of the big cathedrals before this time, which had their own headquarters, their own administrators, their own artisans or artists as part of the organization. The structure which was concerned with the new St. Peter's under Julius II, on the contrary, was strictly oligarchical, the individuals in charge could clearly be distinguished, and everything depended on the pontiff for final approval. Even the architect had no assistant, or better, he had to pay his assistants from his own pocket: first Antonio di Pellegrino, then Antonio da Sangallo the Younger. Thanks to this organizational simplicity, it is possible – without too much effort – to reconstruct the financial commitment of the enterprise, since, in the early years, all the contracts with the workers, and all the amounts accredited to the bank of Ghinucci were recorded in the *Liber Mandatorum*, a small volume originally of eighty pages. We can thus trace the flow of expenses, which corresponded to the progress of the construction yard: in the first year, 1506, the total came to 12,500 ducats; in the next year, 27,200 ducats; in the years immediately following, 14,300 (1508), 13,438 (1509) and 14,391 ducats (1510), respectively. From 1511 until the death of Julius II in the beginning of 1513, the financing of the construction slowed down a great deal, almost to the point of stopping. There was certainly a connection with the greater military expenses sustained by the State and the personal coffers of the pontiff, but there was probably also less interest on the part of the pope, who had apparently lost interest because of the economic needs of the undertaking, which, despite the fact that work had progressed, was still very far from being finished. In order to find the funds necessary for what he thought was one of the most important needs of all of Christianity, Julius II even resorted to going beyond his own funds and those of the funds of the Camera Apostolica by appealing to the generosity of Europe. Already in February of 1507, he had signed a bull which conceded indulgences to anyone who donated whatever money possible, to be left in a locked chest in St. Peter's. Two months later, he imposed a tribute on all ecclesiastical possessions with the payment of one tenth destined for the construction of the basilica. Through the preachers of the different reli-

Monotonie im Entwurf des Florentiners. Auf geniale Weise fügt er in den seitlichen Räumen Umgänge ein, die auf phantasiereichere Art den Raum hierarchisieren sollten, indem der von der großen Kuppel beherrschte Bereich von den kleineren unterschieden wurde. Oben auf dem Blatt befindet sich der rasch skizzierte Grundriß von San Lorenzo in Mailand; dieser spätantike Bau stellte ein typisches Beispiel für die Verwendung von Umgängen dar. Es scheint, als ob Bramante sich bei der hitzigen Diskussion mit dem Papst und seinem Konkurrenten mit einem Zitat aus dem Altertum hätte rechtfertigen müssen.

Wenn bisher die Zeichnung als Kommunikationsmittel zwischen den Architekten und ihrem Auftraggeber oder untereinander betrachtet worden ist, so gibt es genügend andere Zeichnungen, die als eigene Entwürfe entstanden sind und die man als Diskussion des Architekten mit sich selbst verstehen könnte. Beispielsweise ist die UA20 ein recht großer Papierbogen (684 x 470 mm), auf dem mit Rötelstift die Linienzüge auf einem dichten Raster aus kleinen Quadraten gezeichnet sind; jede Einheit (3,7 mm) entsprach 5 römischen „Palmi" bzw. 112 cm. Dieses Raster wurde mit Tinte angefertigt, damit der Architekt, auch wenn er freihändig zeichnete, sofort einen maßstabgerechten Vergleich hatte. Mit Tinte wurde auch der Grundriß der alten Basilika gezeichnet, um die Ausmaße des zu planenden Bauwerks besser mit den schon bestehenden vergleichen zu können. Während der Arbeit muß sich der Bogen dann als unzureichend erwiesen haben, da am linken Rand ein schmaler Papierstreifen angestückt wurde. Die Linienführung ist hier vollkommen anders als bei den eleganten und sorgfältig ausgeführten Präsentationszeichnungen. Die Vorgehensweise des Architekten mit teilweise doppelt nachgezogenen Linien scheint auf die brennende Suche nach einer Lösung hinzuweisen. Beim genauen Hinsehen lassen sich zwei unterschiedliche Ideen auf dem Blatt ausmachen, oder vielmehr die Entstehung einer Idee aus der anderen. Man braucht nur die vier Pfeiler zu betrachten, die die große Hauptkuppel stützen sollten. Der nordöstliche Pfeiler besitzt deutlich geringere Ausmaße als die übrigen drei, die offensichtlich gleich danach gezeichnet wurden, um eine oder besser mehrere Möglichkeiten auszuprobieren, denn trotz ihrer Ähnlichkeit sind sie unterschiedlich. Dabei sollten die Nischen durch die Vergrößerung der Pfeiler anders gestaltet werden. Auf diese Weise enthalten die vier Quadranten des Grundrisses unterschiedliche Lösungsvorschläge. Oben studiert der Architekt mit zügigen Linien, die er freihändig ausführt, den Aufriß des Innenraums der Basilika, während auf der Rückseite ebenfalls skizzenhaft der Aufriß der Außenansicht und der Grundriß der Kuppel dargestellt sind.

Diesem ausschließlich zum persönlichen Gebrauch bestimmten Blatt steht die nach Baubeginn angefertigte Zeichnung UA6770 gegenüber, auf der Bramante den Steinmetzen die Form der Kapitelle der großen inneren Säulenordnung vermittelte. Im Maßstab 1:5 führte er teilweise freihändig, teilweise mit Zirkel und Lineal eine „Ausführungszeichnung" aus, wie wir sie heute nennen würden, d. h. die Zeichnung war für die Ausführenden

gious orders, he appealed to the faithful; he went to see rulers in person to ask for the necessary funds, promising absolution from sins in exchange for the necessary funds to make the grandeur of the vicar of Christ architecturally visible on earth. But, upon his death in February 1513, the state of construction was far from being finished: the four great piers on which the dome was supposed to rest were only as far as the pendentives; the arm of the choir only reached the springer of the vault; the two piers of the central nave stuck out of the foundations.

The simple working structure desired by Julius II, who could immediately tell who the individuals in charge of the project were, began to become complicated after his death. The new pope, the Florentine Leo X (1513–1521), a Medici, was young (barely thirty-seven) and ambitious. The son of Lorenzo il Magnifico, he had also inherited the habit of dealing with artists and the fame of a great patron of the arts. If, on the one hand, he understood that the project of 1506 would require more time than Julius II had estimated, on the other, he wanted a basilica with truly colossal dimensions. With an eye toward prolonging the construction, he asked Bramante to cover whatever had been constructed, and decided to create an organizational structure equipped to last for a long time, which evidently did not scare the young pontiff. The elderly Bramante was joined by Fra Giocondo, who was also very old, in the role of advisor in November 1513. Although nearly eighty, Fra Giocondo's technical training must have been invaluable. From January 1514 on, Giuliano da Sangallo, the Medici family architect, began to create a stable organization for construction, thanks to the greater availability of funds that were soon translated more into salaries for collaborators than into progress on the work, and more in "agreements" for supplies than in construction.

As soon as he was elected, he asked for a new, more expansive project which would not stop even at the idea of remodelling whatever had already been constructed, or at the preservation of the Early Christian basilica. Writing in 1540, a theorist of the Cinquecento, Sebastiano Serlio, attributed to this period the idea of a grandiose dome which would coordinate the entire building. But, hardly one year after Julius II, Bramante, too, died, and the problem of finding a successor arose. Many very talented architects could have thought of taking on the project, which was the most prestigious in the Eternal City. Apart from the two elderly artists that Leo X had summoned to help Bramante, the promising young Antonio da Sangallo was active in the construction. He was an expert architect who received his training in the construction yard of St. Peter's, gradually taking on jobs of increasing importance. In the summer of 1514, Leo X went outside the *Fabbrica* for his choice, and chose – perhaps upon the advice of the dying Bramante – the most famous artist of the time, Raphael Sanzio, who was almost entirely without any practical experience in architecture. A friend and fellow Urbinate,

bestimmt, wobei nur der zum Verständnis seitens der Steinmetze notwendige Teil dargestellt wurde.

Das Bedürfnis der Architekten, mit dem Auftraggeber, den ausführenden Kräften oder untereinander zu kommunizieren, sich unterschiedliche Lösungen vorzustellen – und das an einem Bauplatz, dessen Ausmaße bei weitem alle Unternehmungen übertraf, die die Renaissancearchitektur bisher verwirklicht hatte –, all diese Faktoren führten zwangsläufig dazu, die Zeichnung an die neuen Anforderungen anzupassen, über ihre bisherigen Grenzen hinauszugehen und sie als dialektisches Mittel zu benutzen. Wenn auch nicht der Beruf des Architekten, so ist jedoch die Zeichnung als Hauptinstrument der Architektur die wesentliche Hinterlassenschaft der neuentworfenen Peterskirche.

Auch bei der Organisation und der Finanzierung des Bauwerks stellte Julius II. die Abhängigkeit der Basilika von der Rolle des Papstes deutlich in den Vordergrund. Die Kathedralen – als erste die toskanischen und lombardischen – besaßen eine komplizierte, spezifische Struktur, die zur Regelung der mit dem Bau verbundenen Abläufe diente und „Fabbrica" bzw. „Opera" genannt wurde; in ihr spiegelten sich die weltlichen und kirchlichen Ämter der Stadt wider. Außerdem wurden hier die Interessen der unterschiedlichen sozialen Schichten vertreten oder trafen aufeinander. Die neue Peterskirche unterstand jedoch in den ersten Jahren ihrer langen Baugeschichte streng dem Papst und seinem engen Mitarbeiterkreis. Mit der Organisation der Bauhütte beschäftigte sich der „Sacro Palazzo", die für die päpstlichen Residenzen zuständige Behörde; die Geldmittel stammten aus der Apostolischen Kammer und aus der Geheimen Staatskasse des Papstes und damit praktisch aus seiner Privatkasse. Demzufolge waren der Architekt Donato Bramante, der Buchhalter Girolamo di Francesco da Siena und der Vermesser Riniero da Pisa, der die Ausführung der Arbeiten überwachte, auch für die anderen päpstlichen Bauten zuständig. Ebenso standen die Mitarbeiter, die die ansehnlichen Geldmittel für das Bauwerk verwalteten, dem Papst sehr nahe und genossen sein äußerstes Vertrauen, wie zum Beispiel der Kardinal Fabrizio Santoro, der Erzbischof von Taranto Enrico Bruni und nach dessen Tod im Jahr 1509 Orlando del Carretto sowie Bartolomeo Ferratini. Auch die Zahlungen wurden von einem der zahlreichen Bankiers, die für Julius II. arbeiteten, dem aus Siena stammenden Stefano Ghinucci, ausgeführt. Dies alles hatte mit der Organisationsstruktur der Bauhütte einer Kathedrale aus früherer Zeit, die in der Regel über einen eigenen Sitz, eigene Verwalter, Handwerker und Künstler verfügte, kaum etwas zu tun. Im Gegensatz dazu war die Organisationsstruktur, die unter der Leitung von Julius II. für die neue Peterskirche zuständig war, streng vertikal aufgebaut; es hoben sich deutlich die einzelnen Verantwortungsbereiche ab, und alles unterstand der letzten Instanz, dem Papst. Der Architekt hatte noch nicht einmal einen Assistenten, vielmehr mußte er aus eigener Tasche seine Mitarbeiter bezahlen, wie zunächst Antonio di Pellegrino und später Antonio da Sangallo. Dank der einfach strukturierten Organisation läßt sich der finanzielle Aufwand des Unternehmens leicht

Giuliano da Sangallo, plan of the project for St. Peter's. Florence, Uffizi, Gabinetto Disegni e Stampe, 7A

Giuliano da Sangallo, Grundriß zum Projekt der Peterskirche. Florenz, Uffizien, Gabinetto Disegni e Stampe, 7A

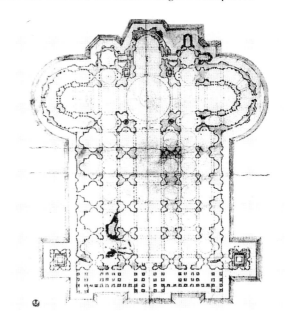

Domenico Aimo da Varignana, copy of Raphael's second project for St. Peter's.
New York, Pierpont Morgan Library, Codex Mellon, f. 72v

Domenico Aimo da Varignana, Kopie des zweiten Entwurfs Raffaels für St. Peter.
New York, Pierpont Morgan Library, Codex Mellon, Folio 72v

like Bramante an expert and restorer of antiquity, to the pope, who had set his eyes on distant goals, he seemed to be the one designated to inherit the position, all the more so, since, in those years, his artistic path went from painting to the creation of a unitary whole composed of the different arts. Perhaps he had just started to "order" – according to the pleasant expression of Vasari – the chapel of Santa Maria del Popolo for the Sienese banker Agostino Chigi, the richest man in Rome. By not going to an "expert" of construction, but to a major artist, Leo X reconfirmed the absolutely representative nature of the basilica. At first, Fra Giocondo and Giuliano da Sangallo had been concerned with technical problems. Then (the former died in July of 1515, and the latter returned to Florence at the same time), Antonio da Sangallo was nominated "second architect" of the construction in December of 1516, and Baldassarre Peruzzi, assistant to Antonio and Raphael. Raphael had two ideas after this. The first, which can be dated to 1514, is almost a continuation of Bramante's ideas, and can be reconstructed thanks to one of Serlio's engravings, a drawing by Giuliano da Sangallo and a sketch, 1973F, in the Uffizi. The second, from 1519, is more mature, and is documented by a drawing attributed to Domenico da Varignana, but in any event worked out in the close Raphaelesque circle, in the Codex Mellon in the Pierpont Morgan Library in New York. Very little was constructed, but certainly the intense formal research of those years had some impact on the successive layout of the basilica. Surely, with Raphael, St. Peter's became, much more than under Bramante, the problem of the architecture of the time, in all of Europe, and not only in Rome. This is clear from the proliferation of copies of projects, of reliefs of what had been constructed or sculpted, in the sketchbooks in which young architects studied the elaborate solutions. But above all, with the nomination of Raphael, for the first time, architectural construction was supposed to reflect the personal "style", or creation of the artist. In these very years, competition among the various artists was institutionalized in the contest system (for the façade of San Lorenzo in Florence, for the new church of the Archconfraternity of Florentines in Rome, to mention only two of many cases) through which patrons could choose from the best projects presented by architects.

The competition among personal *maniere*, or styles, almost reached the level of professional dishonesty, if not downright slander. A sheet in the Uffizi, UA33, shows, beside the sketches representing the plan of the basilica, a sketch in the hand of Antonio da Sangallo of a sort of memorandum to the pope on the errors committed in the construction of St. Peter's. It says: "Mosso piu a miserichordia e onore di Dio e di Santo Pietro e onore e utile di Vostra Santità che a utilità mia per fare intendere chome li danari che si spendono chon pocho onore e utile di Dio e di Vostra Santità perche sono buttati via le chagioni sono queste infaschritte" (Acting more out of pity and respect for God and St. Peter and respect and the desire to be useful to Your Holi-

rekonstruieren: In den Anfangsjahren wurden alle Verträge, die mit den Arbeitern abgeschlossen wurden, und alle auf die Ghinucci-Bank überwiesenen Geldsummen in dem „Liber Mandatorum" registriert, einem kleinen Buch mit ursprünglich 80 Seiten. Dadurch lassen sich die Ausgaben in Übereinstimmung mit dem Verlauf der Bauarbeiten verfolgen, die sich im ersten Jahr (1506) auf 12.500 Dukaten beliefen, im nächsten auf 27.200 Dukaten und in den unmittelbar darauffolgenden auf 14.300 (1508), 13.438 (1509) und 14.391 Dukaten (1510). Von 1511 bis zum Tod Julius' II. Anfang 1513 verlangsamte sich der Fluß der Finanzierungsmittel erheblich und kam beinahe zum Stillstand. Dies hing sicherlich mit den erhöhten Militärausgaben des Staates und der persönlichen Kasse des Papstes zusammen, aber auch mit einem verringerten Interesse Julius' II., der aufgrund der finanziellen Anforderungen des Unternehmens, das trotz der fortschreitenden Arbeiten noch sehr weit von seiner Fertigstellung entfernt war, offensichtlich entmutigt war. Um die notwendigen Geldmittel für das Projekt zu beschaffen, das er als wichtigstes Bedürfnis der gesamten Christenheit ansah, hatte Julius II. nicht nur auf seine eigenen Möglichkeiten und auf die Geldmittel der Apostolischen Kammer zurückgegriffen, sondern sich auch die Großzügigkeit ganz Europas zunutze gemacht. Bereits im Februar 1507 hatte er eine Bulle unterzeichnet, mit der er denjenigen einen Ablaß erteilte, die in einer verschlossenen Schatulle in St. Peter soviel gespendet hätten, wie ihnen ihre frommen Seelen ermöglichten. Zwei Monate später hatte er allen kirchlichen Besitztümern die Abgabe eines Zehnten auferlegt, der für den Bau der neuen Basilika bestimmt war. Mit Hilfe von Predigern unterschiedlicher Ordensgemeinschaften hatte er sich an die Gläubigen und persönlich an die Herrscher gewandt, um die notwendigen Geldmittel zu erbitten. Als Gegenleistung für die Spenden, mit denen die Größe des Stellvertreters Christi auf Erden architektonisch sichtbar gemacht werden sollte, versicherte er ihnen die Lossprechung von ihren Sünden. Als Julius II. im Februar 1513 starb, lag die Vollendung des Bauwerks noch in weiter Ferne: Die vier großen Pfeiler, auf denen die Kuppel ruhen sollte, hatten die Höhe der Zwickel erreicht, der Chor war bis zum Gewölbe ausgeführt, und die beiden Pfeiler des Mittelschiffs ragten gerade aus ihren Sockeln hervor.

Die klare und einfache von Julius II. geschaffene Arbeitsstruktur, die unmittelbar die einzelnen Verantwortlichen für das Projekt benannte, verkomplizierte sich nach seinem Tod. Der neue Papst, der Florentiner Leo X. (1513–1521) aus der Familie Medici, war jung – er war gerade 37 Jahre alt – und ehrgeizig. Als Sohn Lorenzos il Magnifico hatte er dessen Umgang mit Künstlern und den Ruf eines großen Mäzens geerbt. Auch wenn er einerseits einsah, daß für das Projekt aus dem Jahr 1506 sehr viel mehr Zeit als von Julius II. vorgesehen nötig gewesen wäre, wollte er eine Basilika mit gewaltigen Ausmaßen verwirklichen. Er forderte Bramante auf, das bisher Errichtete in Anbetracht der Verlängerung der Bauzeit zu überdecken, und beschloß, eine Organisationsstruktur aufzubauen, die

ness, than to myself, this is to inform you how the money being spent with little respect for or use to God and Your Holiness is like throwing money away, and the reasons are written down here), and a long list of linguistic and technical errors present in the project follows. It is not difficult to recognize it as Raphael's second project. Since it is unthinkable that such a ferocious attack might be written when the artist was still alive, scholars have dated the memo to the days immediately following the death of the "divine" Raphael, whose untimely death – in April 1520, at only thirty-seven – had caused not only universal mourning, but also had heightened the sense of rivalry among his possible successors. It is impossible to know if the memo – which on the Uffizi sheet seems to be a mere sketch – was ever given to the pontiff. Hence we cannot tell whether these criticisms addressed to the one who had wanted him, Sangallo, as main assistant to the object of those criticisms, had any weight in Leo X's decision to have him replace Raphael in the position of "main architect". However, it is certain that the criticisms and the accusations of bad use of the funds collected from all of Christianity – which could be added to those of Guarna to Bramante in 1517, those of the Northern humanists, and the protests of princes who saw their precious national resources drained off to Rome – must have convinced Leo X, in 1520, to entrust to Sangallo and Peruzzi, in competition between the two, the task of drawing up yet another project. This time it was to be in the form of a wooden model, and cut the economic commitment down to size. Both models have been lost, but from engravings by Serlio it is clear that Peruzzi's project – in August 1520 "second architect" of St. Peter's – took up Raphaelesque ideas, inserting them in the centric system unsuccessfully proposed by Bramante to Julius II. Instead, from Jean de Chenevières' relief of Sangallo's model, it seems that he – by using his own knowledge of the building and its history, and renewing the offer of his conscientious and professional functionalism – sacrificed the complex balance studied by Bramante and Raphael, simplifying it, but saving the longitudinal layout to which the construction was committed. The opposite poles of Sangallo's professionality, which was based on the imposing and costly machine which directed and governed the work, and the imaginative re-elaboration of Bramante's and Raphael's projects was to characterize the entire second decade of the century, marked as it was by the irregular progress of the work, caused by the death of Leo X (1521), who was succeeded by the austere, prudent Hadrian VI (1521–1523), from Flanders, and hence a stranger to Roman culture. Only with the elevation to the throne of Clement VII, another Medici, was work vigorously taken up again. But Clementine magnificence in Rome, which witnessed the flowering of the bizarre eccentricity of Rosso, the refined elegance of Parmigianino, and the dominance of the workshop of Raphael, was soon interrupted in 1527 by dramatic historical events.

auf lange Dauer ausgelegt war, was den jungen Papst offensichtlich nicht erschreckte. Dem betagten Bramante stellte er im November 1513 als Berater den greisen Fra Giocondo zur Seite, der mittlerweile 80 Jahre alt war, aber dessen fachliche Erfahrung sehr wertvoll sein konnte. Im Januar 1514 kam Giuliano da Sangallo, der Architekt der Medici, hinzu. Er begann mit der Einrichtung einer festen Organisationsstruktur der Bauhütte, die auch dank der besseren finanziellen Situation ermöglicht wurde. Die Geldmittel wurden allerdings schon sehr bald in höhere Gehälter für die Mitarbeiter statt in ein Vorankommen der Arbeiten und eher in „Abkommen" für die Lieferung der Materialien als in den eigentlichen Bau investiert.

Kurz nach seiner Wahl forderte Leo X. einen neuen, größeren Entwurf, der auch nicht vor einer Umarbeitung des bisher Gebauten oder vor der Erhaltung der frühchristlichen Basilika Halt machen sollte. Sebastiano Serlio, ein Architekturtheoretiker des 16. Jahrhunderts, schrieb 1540, daß aus jener Zeit die Idee der großartigen Kuppel stamme, die den Gesamtbau in Einklang bringen sollte. Aber kaum ein Jahr nach dem Tod Julius' II. starb auch Bramante, womit sich das Problem seines Nachfolgers stellte. Es gab zahlreiche bedeutende Architekten, die dieses Amt, das prestigeträchtigste der Ewigen Stadt, anstreben konnten. Außer den beiden alten Künstlern, die Leo X. Bramante zur Seite gestellt hatte, war in der Bauhütte auch der junge, hervorragende Antonio da Sangallo tätig, ein fachkundiger Architekt, der seine Erfahrung in der Bauhütte gesammelt hatte und im Laufe der Zeit mit immer anspruchsvolleren Aufgaben betraut worden war. Die Wahl Leos X. fiel jedoch im Sommer 1514, möglicherweise auf den Rat des sterbenden Bramante hin, auf Raffael, den berühmtesten Künstler jener Jahre, der im Architekturbereich nahezu keine Erfahrung besaß. Der Freund und Landsmann Bramantes, der wie der Architekt ein Kenner und Nachahmer der Antike war, schien in den weitsichtigen Augen des Papstes dieser Aufgabe gewachsen zu sein, insbesondere, da sich seine künstlerische Laufbahn gerade in jenen Jahren von der Malerei abwandte, um eine Ganzheit zu schaffen, in der die verschiedenen Künste zusammenflossen. Er hatte vielleicht gerade erst begonnen, die Kapelle in Santa Maria del Popolo für Agostino Chigi, den Bankier aus Siena und reichsten Mann Roms, zu „ordnen", wie der glückliche Ausdruck Vasaris besagt. Die Entscheidung Leos X., sich nicht an einen „Baufachmann" zu wenden, sondern an einen berühmten Künstler, unterstreicht den rein repräsentativen Charakter der Basilika. Mit den technischen Problemen beschäftigten sich zunächst Fra Giocondo und Giuliano da Sangallo; nach dem Tod Fra Giocondos im Juli 1515 und der gleichzeitigen Rückkehr Sangallos nach Florenz wurde Antonio da Sangallo im Dezember 1516 zum „zweiten Architekten" der Bauhütte ernannt; mit ihm arbeitete Baldassarre Peruzzi, der auch der Assistent Raffaels war. Raffael sind zwei Entwürfe zu verdanken. Der erste, aus dem Jahr 1514, der geradezu eine Fortsetzung der Ideen Bramantes darstellt, kann dank eines Stichs von Serlio, der Zeichnungen Giulianos da Sangallo und der Skizze 1973F in den Uffizien rekonstruiert werden. Der zweite, reifere

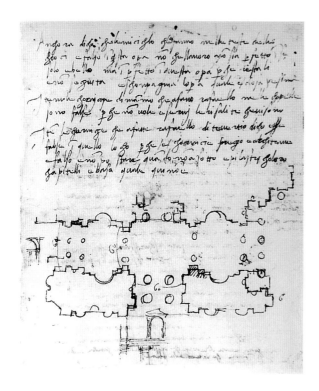

Antonio da Sangallo the Younger, sketch for memorandum on the progress of the construction of St. Peter's, with studies of plans and view of the pronaos.
Florence, Uffizi, Gabinetto Disegni e Stampe, 33Av

Antonio da Sangallo d. J., Entwurf für eine Bittschrift zum Bauverlauf der Peterskirche mit Studien zum Grundriß und zur Fassade der Vorhalle.
Florenz, Uffizien, Gabinetto Disegni e Stampe, 33Av

We do not know whether the criticisms in Sangallo's memo were what made Leo X re-dimension the grandiose projects for St. Peter's. In any event, other criticisms, whose historical importance was undoubtedly initially underestimated in Rome, came from Germany, where, in 1517, precisely to raise objections to the preachers in Wittenberg and Brandenburg who were promising indulgences for whoever made an offering to St. Peter's, an obscure Saxon Augustinian monk, Martin Luther, threw into question the Catholic theory of salvation by means of works, and wrote: "The pope cannot and does not intend to remit more sins, if not those he himself has imposed, through his own authority and the authority of canonic law". And later: "Unless they are rich enough, Christians should use what they have for their families' needs" (fifth and sixty-seventh of the ninety-five so-called Wittenberg theses, because they were traditionally thought to have been nailed to the doors of the church of that city). Obviously, Luther's theses, and those of his first disciples, merely took their inspiration from the reconstruction of the new basilica of St. Peter's (the Saxon monk could have seen it during the four weeks he spent in Rome between the end of 1510 and the first days of 1511) in order to deny the possibility of a Christian's securing salvation through his works and not his faith, reject the authority of the pontiff and preach a more individual relationship with God thanks to the reading of the Bible in the vernacular. They thus systematically took up again and re-elaborated spiritual tendencies present throughout the Middle Ages. But the controversy over the luxury and corruption of the Roman clergy, over the veneration of relics and the cult of the saints as mediators in salvation and over the supremacy of the pope were certainly better weapons for the spread of Protestantism, as is clear from the many satirical inscriptions aimed at the court of Rome, the rich prelates, and corrupt clergy. In just a few years, the evangelical message spread like wildfire in all of Northern Europe, in Germany, in Scandinavia, in England, in Switzerland, in France, in the Low Countries: and barely ten years after the diffusion of the ninety-five theses of Luther, in 1527, with the terrible Sack by the Lanzichenecchi, Rome herself experienced the horrors of war, worsened by hate and religious intolerance.

Rome emerged from the terrible experience of the Sack transformed: she had seen soldiers make fun of the pope, humiliate him, kill prelates and sack the churches and wealthy residences of the city, profane relics, and express their hate for the Eternal City – the New Babylon, the seat of all vices – in a thousand ways. When Protestantism began to take hold, and also after the tendencies, in the Catholic community itself, towards reform of the Church, the progress of the construction yard of the new basilica of St. Peter's became not only an architectural but also a moral problem. Clement VII never got over the humiliation of the Sack, and in 1531, he asked Sangallo and Peruzzi to scale down the project for St. Peter's again. He was succeeded by Alessandro Farnese, who took the name of Paul III

Entwurf aus dem Jahr 1519 ist in einer Zeichnung dokumentiert, die im „Codex Mellon" der Pierpont Morgan Library in New York Domenico da Varignana zugeschrieben wird, jedenfalls aber im engen Mitarbeiterkreis Raffaels ausgeführt wurde. Von diesen Entwürfen wurde nur wenig realisiert, jedoch beeinflußte die intensive formale Suche die nachfolgende Anlage der Basilka. Mit Sicherheit wurde St. Peter unter Raffaels Leitung – und das in sehr viel stärkerem Maße als unter Bramante – zu einem Problem der zeitgenössischen europäischen und nicht nur der römischen Architektur. Dies belegen die immer zahlreicheren Kopien der Entwürfe und die Beobachtungen dessen, was gebaut oder gehauen war, in den Skizzenbüchern junger Architekten, die sich mit den erarbeiteten Lösungen auseinandersetzten. Vor allem aber wird mit der Ernennung Raffaels zum ersten Mal ganz deutlich, daß das Bauwerk den persönlichen „Stil", die Erfindung des Künstlers widerspiegelt. In jenen Jahren wurde die Konkurrenz der Künstler untereinander durch Wettbewerbe institutionalisiert (beispielsweise für die Fassade von San Lorenzo in Florenz und die neue Kirche der Erzbruderschaft der Florentiner in Rom), anhand derer die Auftraggeber die besten, von den Architekten vorgelegten Entwürfe auswählten.

Die Konkurrenz der persönlichen „Stile" konnte auch zu Unfairneß führen, wenn nicht sogar zu offener Verleumdung. Auf dem Blatt UA33 in den Uffizien ist neben den Skizzen Antonios da Sangallo, die den Grundriß der Basilika darstellen, der Entwurf einer Art Bittschrift zu sehen, die an den Papst gerichtet ist und die in St. Peter begangenen Fehler betrifft. Darin heißt es: „Ich denke vielmehr an das Erbarmen und die Ehre Gottes und des heiligen Petrus und an die Ehre und den Nutzen Eurer Heiligkeit als an mein eigenes Interesse, wenn ich davon unterrichte, wie die Gelder mit wenig Ehre und Nutzen Gott und Eurer Heiligkeit gegenüber ausgegeben werden, da sie verschleudert werden." Dann folgt eine lange Auflistung der technischen und strukturellen Fehler des Projekts, das man leicht als den zweiten Entwurf Raffaels erkennen kann. Da es kaum denkbar ist, daß eine so scharfe Kritik an den noch lebenden Künstler gerichtet war, hat die Kunstgeschichte die Schrift in die Tage unmittelbar nach dem frühen Tod des „göttlichen" Raffael im April 1520 im Alter von nur 37 Jahren datiert, der allgemeine Trauer erregte, aber auch die Rivalität zwischen seinen möglichen Nachfolgern zuspitzte. Es ist nicht in Erfahrung zu bringen, ob die Bittschrift, die auf dem Blatt der Uffizien nur im Entwurf niedergeschrieben zu sein scheint, jemals dem Papst übergeben wurde. Daher läßt sich auch nicht beurteilen, ob Sangallos Kritik an Raffael in irgendeiner Weise bei der Entscheidung Leos X., Antonio im Amt des „ersten Architekten" als Nachfolger Raffaels zu bestimmen, ins Gewicht gefallen ist. Sicherlich aber haben die Kritiken und Klagen über den Mißbrauch der in der gesamten Christenheit gesammelten Geldmittel, zu denen nach den an Bramante gerichteten Anschuldigungen Guarnas 1517 die der nordischen Humanisten sowie die Proteste der Fürsten, die ihre Landesfinanzen zugunsten Roms gedrosselt sahen, hinzukamen, Leo X. davon überzeugt,

(1534–1549). An energetic Roman cardinal who based the program of his pontificate on a profound reform of the Church, he initiated the Council of Trent, through which, on the one hand, he wanted to re-assert the orthodoxy of Catholic doctrine, while on the other, to attempt a reconciliation with those who had taken distance from the Church, and to reform and purify the customs of the religious. The determination of a definitive project for the basilica, and its frightfully unestimated costs, were among the points that most worried him. In the frescoes which celebrate – live, as they were happening – his undertakings, in Castel Sant'Angelo as in the Palazzo della Cancelleria, he tries to systematically define himself as the founder of the new St. Peter's. Shortly after having been elected, he brought Peruzzi's pay to the same level as Sangallo's, and asked both to clearly draw up a definitive project. UA2, the famous project in bird's-eye perspective prepared by Peruzzi for the pontiff, is the most brilliant demonstration of how far architectural drawing had come in the laborious attempt at communication between architects and patrons in the history of the construction of St. Peter's. But in 1539, as far as the ultimate definition of the form of the basilica and all its constructive details is concerned, since Peruzzi had died in 1536 and left Sangallo alone, it is significant that reference was made to a large model in wood, of extraordinary dimensions (over seven meters long and six high, on a scale of 1:30) and as expensive – or so says Vasari – as a small church. This prodigy of the representative technique of architecture was created in seven long years by the carpenter-architect Labacco following the very detailed drawings by Antonio da Sangallo. It was so urgently wished for by Paul III as to cause him to threaten the architect with the suspension of this monthly salary if the model was not turned over ("quoad architectos salaria mandarunt non satisfieri nisi incepto modello", as decided the assembly of the *Fabbrica* in June of 1539). It sums up, in effect, thirty years of plans, and was a job which only the excellent expert trained in the construction yards of St. Peter's could have undertaken, since he had personally known all of the great leading figures who had been in charge of it. In the control of the construction yard, its suppliers and the workers employed there, he found the strength to become the dominant figure on the Roman artistic scene. The great model in wood, however, was both his most mature project and his spiritual legacy.

The last payments to Labacco are in August of 1546. In September, Antonio da Sangallo died suddenly, after twenty-six years of service on the construction as "first architect". Obviously, a vacuum which was difficult to fill was created: no one else could boast the detailed knowledge of all the complex links in such a highly articulated construction yard. The deputies of the *Fabbrica* had thought of substituting him with the favorite disciple of Raphael, Giulio Romano. He had soon left Rome, and moved to the court of the Gonzaga in 1524, and at Mantova he had become one of the great expo-

1520 Sangallo und Peruzzi, in Konkurrenz zueinander, einen weiteren Entwurf anfertigen zu lassen. Diesmal sollte er jedoch als Holzmodell ausgeführt werden und ebenso darauf bedacht sein, den vorgesehenen finanziellen Aufwand zu reduzieren. Beide Modelle sind verlorengegangen. Allerdings läßt sich aus den Stichen Serlios ersehen, daß Peruzzi, der im August 1520 „zweiter Architekt" war, die Ideen Raffaels aufgriff und in das Zentralbauprojekt einfügte, das Bramante Julius II. ohne Erfolg vorgeschlagen hatte. Aus Jean de Chenevières' Aufmaß des Modells von Sangallo wird hingegen deutlich, daß dieser sich seine Kenntnis des Bauwerks und dessen Geschichte zunutze gemacht hatte und wiederum eine bewußt professionelle Funktionalität vorschlug. Durch die Vereinfachung verzichtete er auf das komplexe Gleichgewicht, das Bramante und Raffael erarbeitet hatten, auch wenn er die Längsausrichtung des Bauwerks beibehielt, die der Kirche nunmehr zugrunde lag. Der Gegensatz zwischen der professionellen Korrektheit Sangallos, die sich auf die mächtige und kostspielige Bauorganisation stützte, welche die Arbeiten leitete und beaufsichtigte, und der phantasievollen Ausarbeitung der Pläne Bramantes und später Raffaels sollte die gesamten 20er Jahre des Jahrhunderts prägen. In dieser Zeit kamen die Arbeiten dennoch nur schleppend voran, was mit dem Tod Leos X. (1521) zusammenhing. Sein Nachfolger, der ernste und vorsichtige Niederländer Hadrian VI. (1521–1523), stand der römischen Kultur eher fremd gegenüber. Erst mit der Wahl Clemens' VII., ebenfalls ein Medici, wurden die Arbeiten wieder aufgenommen. Die clementinische Zeit der Pracht, die in Rom die Exzentrik Rosso Fiorentinos, die erlesene Eleganz Parmigianinos und die Vorherrschaft der Schüler Raffaels hervorbrachte, wurde jedoch schon 1527 von dramatischen historischen Ereignissen unterbrochen.

Ob die in der Bittschrift Sangallos vorgebrachte Kritik Leo X. überzeugt hat, die großangelegten Entwürfe für St. Peter einzugrenzen, wissen wir nicht. Weitere Kritik historischer Relevanz, die in Rom anfänglich zweifellos unterschätzt wurde, kam jedoch aus Deutschland. Dort hatte 1517 ein unbekannter Augustinermönch aus Sachsen namens Martin Luther die katholische Lehre, das Heil sei durch Werke zu erlangen, in Frage gestellt. Er widersetzte sich insbesondere den Predigern, die in Wittenberg und Brandenburg denjenigen den Sündenablaß versprachen, die eine kleine Gabe für St. Peter gespendet hätten. Luther schrieb: „Der Papst kann und beabsichtigt nicht neue Strafen zu erlassen, außer denjenigen, die er selbst mit seiner Autorität und der Autorität des kanonischen Rechts auferlegt hat", und weiter: „Es sei denn, die Christen verfügen über überflüssige Reichtümer, ansonsten sollen sie ihren Besitz für die Bedürfnisse ihrer Familien verwenden anstatt damit Ablaßbriefe zu kaufen" (5. und 67. der 95 Thesen an der Wittenberger Schloßkirche). Natürlich diente der Neubau der Peterskirche – der sächsische Mönch hatte sie bei seinem vierwöchigen Romaufenthalt (Ende 1510/ Anfang 1511) gesehen – den Thesen Luthers und seiner ersten Anhänger lediglich als Ausgangspunkt, um die

Plan of the wooden model of St. Peter's, executed by
Antonio Labacco after the project by Antonio da
Sangallo the Younger, published in Filippo Bonanni,
*Numismata Pontificum Romanorum Templi Vaticani
Fabbricam indicantia,* second edition, Rome 1715,
tav. 14

Grundriß des Holzmodells der Peterskirche, von
Antonio Labacco nach Plänen von Antonio da Sangallo
d. J. ausgeführt, aus: Filippo Bonanni, *Numismata
Pontificum Romanorum Templi Vaticani Fabbricam
indicantia,* 2. Auflage, Rom 1715, Tafel 14

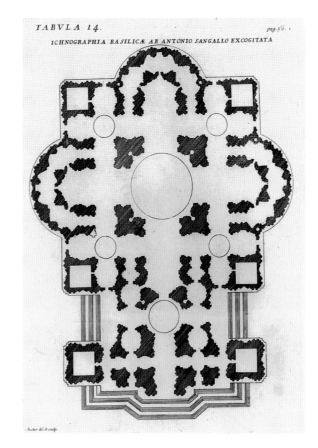

TABVLA 14.   pag.56.

ICHNOGRAPHIA BASILICÆ AB ANTONIO SANGALLO EXCOGITATA

Baldassarre Peruzzi, project in bird's-eye view
perspective.
Florence, Uffizi, Gabinetto Disegni e Stampe, 2A

Baldassarre Peruzzi, Entwurf aus der Vogelperspektive.
Florenz, Uffizien, Gabinetto Disegni e Stampe, 2A

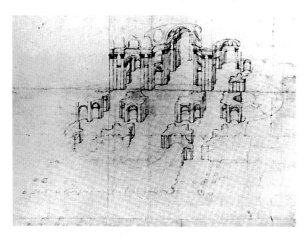

nents of the figurative culture of the time. But the artist
may not have even known about the prestigious position, because he, too, died on 1 November, 1546. In
the second half of November, Paul III – with an act
of dominion overriding the powers of the *Fabbrica* –
decided to assign the position to Michelangelo. Later,
Buonarroti writes in a letter that he was forced by the
pope to take over the construction ("contro mia voglia
con grandissima forza messo da papa Pagolo nella
fabbrica di San Pietro"). His reluctance is justified: the
elderly artist was already over seventy by then, and had
had very little experience in the construction yard. He
had never had much respect for Sangallo, whom he
thought to be a mediocre, even if adequate, professional
in the field of architecture. He did not trust the *Fabbrica*,
which was dominated by disciples, collaborators, and
even relatives of Sangallo. The existence of the wooden
model, which had cost so much, was a guarantee of
continuity, and did not permit further modifications.
Yet he could not refuse: he felt as though the problem
of St. Peter's were his own personal religious problem.
He was close to the Catholic reformers, and had always
kept his distance from the Curia. With St. Peter's, he
took it upon himself and his conscience to deal with the
problem of representation not so much of the role of
the pontiff as that of the Church, just as he had taken
on the harrowing problem – for all souls – of salvation
in the Last Judgement. On the other hand, by confer-
ring the position on Michelangelo, it would have been
impossible for Paul III not to realize that he would be caus-
ing a deep split in the continuity of the construction.

Rechtfertigung allein aus dem Glauben und nicht durch
Werke zu begründen. Zudem bestritt er die Autorität des
Papstes und forderte eine individuellere Beziehung zu
Gott durch die Lektüre der Bibel in der Volkssprache,
wobei er systematisch auf spirituelle Tendenzen, die im
gesamten Mittelalter vorgeherrscht hatten, zurückgriff
und sie ausarbeitete. Aber sicherlich waren die Polemik
gegen den Luxus und die Korruption des römischen
Klerus, gegen die Reliquienverehrung und den Heiligen-
kult als Heilsvermittler sowie gegen die Vormachtstellung
des Papstes die geeignetsten Waffen zur Verbreitung des
Protestantismus, wie die zahlreichen satirischen Drucke
verdeutlichen, die über den römischen Hof, die reichen
Prälaten und den korrupten Klerus spotten. Innerhalb
weniger Jahre verbreitete sich die protestantische Bot-
schaft in ganz Nordeuropa, in Deutschland, Skandina-
vien, England, in der Schweiz, in Frankreich und in den
Niederlanden. Kaum zehn Jahre später bekam Rom bei dem
furchtbaren Sacco di Roma den Kriegsschrecken der
Landsknechte zu spüren, die voller Haß und religiöser
Intoleranz agierten.

Aus der verheerenden Erfahrung des Sacco ging Rom
verwandelt hervor. Es hatte Soldaten erlebt, die mit dem
Papst ihren Spott trieben und ihn demütigten, Prälaten
töteten und Kirchen und reiche Residenzen plünderten,
Reliquien schändeten und auf unterschiedlichste Art und
Weise ihrem Haß gegen die Ewige Stadt, die als das neue
Babylon, als Stätte aller Laster galt, freien Lauf ließen.
Seitdem der Protestantismus Fuß gefaßt hatte, aber auch
infolge der Reformtendenzen innerhalb der katholischen
Kirche war das Fortschreiten des neuen Basilikabaus nicht
nur zu einem architektonischen, sondern auch zu einem
moralischen Problem geworden. Auf Clemens VII., der
die Demütigung des Sacco nicht überwunden und 1531
von Sangallo und Peruzzi eine zusätzliche Reduzierung
des Projekts für St. Peter verlangt hatte, folgte Alessandro
Farnese, der sich Paul III. (1534–1549) nannte. Dieser ener-
gische römische Kardinal, dessen Pontifikatsprogramm
auf eine grundlegende Erneuerung der Kirche abzielte,
berief das Trienter Konzil ein, das einerseits den Kernbe-
stand der katholischen Lehre bestätigen, andererseits aber
eine Versöhnung mit denjenigen, die sich von der Kirche
entfernt hatten, anstreben sowie Ritus und Liturgie re-
formieren und reinigen sollte. Die Festlegung eines definitiven Projekts für die Basilika und seine unendlichen,
erschreckend hohen Kosten beunruhigten den Papst in
besonderem Maße. Mit den Fresken in der Engelsburg und
im Palazzo della Cancelleria, die seine Taten zu seinen Lebzeiten rühmten, wollte man Paul III. programmatisch als
den Begründer der neuen Peterskirche darstellen. Kurz nach
seiner Wahl glich er das Gehalt Peruzzis an das Sangallos
an und forderte beide auf, einen definitiven Entwurf
vorzulegen. Das Blatt UA2 zeigt den berühmten Entwurf
aus der Vogelperspektive, den Peruzzi für den Papst angefertigt hatte. Es belegt auf hervorragende Weise, welch
große Fortschritte die Bauzeichnung bei dem mühevollen
Versuch der Kommunikation zwischen den Architekten und ihren Auftraggebern in der Baugeschichte von
St. Peter gemacht hatte. Es ist jedoch bezeichnend, daß

He must have understood that the great artist, the last great man in an age which was coming to an end, would have been able to base his claims on art, and not merely on expertise, in taking on the task of defining the project started forty years earlier. Now more than ever, the new basilica of St. Peter's became a political problem, not so much of the representation of the supremacy of the pontiff in Christianity, but of the unity of the Church. And art prepared itself in order to be a powerful weapon in the ideological and religious conflict that had broken out, just as the Church made ready for combat.

The correspondence between Monsignor Archinto, one of the most influential deputies of the *Fabbrica*, in Trento at the time for the work of the Council, and his Roman correspondents allows us to follow the first moves of Michelangelo. On 30 November, the elderly architect fired two of Sangallo's main collaborators, saying that he did not want people in his charge who had been there in Sangallo's time ("che non voleva ... homo et officiale e ministro che fossero stati al tempo del Sangallo"). The day after, he told the assembly of the *Fabbrica* that he did not want to answer to anyone except the pope on the progress in the construction yard. During those same days, he had his assistants show him Sangallo's project, sharply criticizing it and stating, as Vasari says, that with so many elements, it seemed like a Gothic rather than a solid ancient or modern work ("con tanti risalti, aguglie, e tritumi di membri, teneva più dell'opera todesca, che del buon modo antico, o della vaga e bella maniera moderna"). On 25 January, 1547, once his nomination

man nach dem Tod Peruzzis im Jahr 1536 – Sangallo war nun allein – 1539 ein großes Holzmodell mit außergewöhnlichen Ausmaßen (über 7 m lang und 6 m hoch, im Maßstab 1:30) angefertigt hatte, das soviel wie eine kleine Kirche kostete. Dieses Wunderwerk der Darstellung war in sieben Jahren von dem Tischler und Architekten Labacco nach minuziösen Zeichnungen Antonios da Sangallo verwirklicht worden. Paul III. hatte derartig darauf bestanden, daß er dem Architekten mit dem Entzug seines Monatsgehalts gedroht hatte, wenn er ihm das Modell nicht abgeliefert hätte ("quoad architectos salaria mandarunt non satisfieri nisi incepto modello", beschloß die Kongregation der Bauhütte im Juni 1539). Das Holzmodell faßt praktisch 30 Jahre Planungsgeschichte zusammen. Dieses Unternehmen war nur für jenen hervorragenden Fachmann möglich gewesen, der seine Ausbildung in der Bauhütte der Peterskirche erhalten hatte und persönlich alle bedeutendenden Hauptakteure kannte, die ihn angeleitet hatten. Die Kontrolle des Baugeschehens, seiner Lieferanten und Arbeiter hatten ihn zur beherrschenden Figur der römischen Künstlerszene gemacht. Das große Holzmodell war sein ausgereiftester Entwurf und gleichzeitig sein geistiges Vermächtnis.

Die letzten Zahlungen an Labacco erfolgten im August 1546. Im September starb unerwartet Antonio da Sangallo, nachdem er 26 Jahre lang als „erster Architekt" an der Bauhütte tätig gewesen war. Damit entstand eine Lücke, die nur schwer zu füllen war. Kein anderer konnte die genaue Kenntnis aller komplizierter Knotenpunkte der

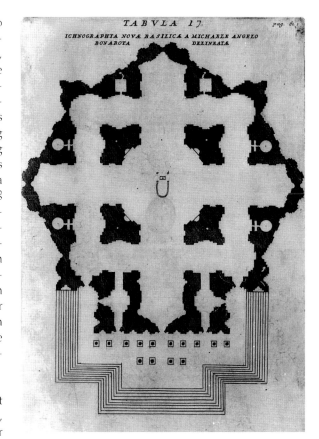

Plan of Michelangelo's project for St. Peter's, published in Filippo Bonanni, *Numismata Pontificum Romanorum Templi Vaticani Fabricam indicantia*, second edition, Rome 1715, tav. 17

Grundriß des Entwurfs Michelangelos für St. Peter, aus: Filippo Bonanni, *Numismata Pontificum Romanorum Templi Vaticani Fabricam indicantia*, 2. Auflage, Rom 1715, Tafel 17

Antonio Salamanca, longitudinal section view toward the south of the model of St. Peter's executed by Antonio Labacco after the project by Antonio da Sangallo the Younger, published in *Speculum Romanae Magnificentiae*, Rome 1575, tav. 146

Antonio Salamanca, in Richtung Süden gesehener Längsschnitt des Modells für St. Peter, das von Antonio Labacco nach Plänen von Antonio da Sangallo d. J. ausgeführt wurde, aus: *Speculum Romanae Magnificentiae*, Rom 1575, Tafel 146

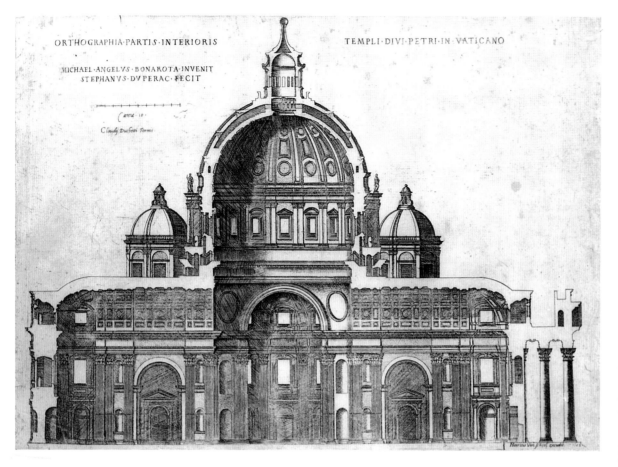

ORTHOGRAPHIA·PARTIS·INTERIORIS   TEMPLI·DIVI·PETRI·IN·VATICANO

MICHAEL·ANGELVS·BONAROTA·INVENIT
STEPHANVS·DVPERAC·FECIT

26

Etienne Dupérac, section of the project
by Michelangelo for St. Peter's

Etienne Dupérac, Querschnitt des Entwurfs
Michelangelos für St. Peter

– for which he wanted no small recompense – had been ratified in writing, he finally took on the deputies of the *Fabbrica*, claiming a privileged, one-to-one relationship with the pontiff and sole responsibility for the direction of the work, concluding, where the deputies might not have understood very well, that he did not want to see fraud or theft in the construction, nor were "deals" to be made with the quarries. Only construction supplies approved by him were to be used ("fare nella fabbrica tanti inganni e roberie, che intendo che il medesimo che è venditore di tevertine, è quello che fa il patto; et non voglio che si muri con altra calcia, pretre et puzolana, che quella che mi piace a me"). We can thus understand the directives of Michelangelo's attack: a return to the single responsibility of Bramante's time and the exclusion of Sangallo's collaborators and the deputies of the *Fabbrica*, whom he suspected of corruption (even in 1557 he justified his refusal to abandon Rome in order not to give them the chance to start stealing again, as was their habit: "non dare ochasione di ritornarvi a rubare, come solevano e ancora spectano i ladri"). The return to Bramante's initial clarity is vindicated by Michelangelo for the project, too. When compared to Sangallo's, the first plan for St. Peter's – he wrote shortly after having accepted the position – was not confusing, but clear and pure, luminous and isolated on all sides. Sangallo's was merely a travesty of Bramante's plan ("non piena di confusione ma chiara e schietta, luminosa e isolata a torno ... e fu tenuta cosa bella, come ancora è manifesto; in modo che chiunche s'è discostato da

Organisation eines dermaßen verwickelten Baus aufweisen. Die Mitglieder der Bauhütte hatten in Erwägung gezogen, ihn durch Giulio Romano, den Lieblingsschüler Raffaels, zu ersetzen, der Rom recht bald verlassen und sich im Oktober 1524 am Hof der Gonzaga niedergelassen hatte. In Mantua galt er als einer der bedeutendsten Vertreter der figurativen Kunst seiner Zeit. Aber vielleicht erfuhr der Künstler noch nicht einmal von dem Vorschlag der prestigeträchtigen Aufgabe, denn auch er starb am 1. November 1546. In der zweiten Novemberhälfte übertrug Paul III. kraft seiner Gewalt, ohne die Zuständigkeit der Bauorganisation zu berücksichtigen, Michelangelo das Amt. Später sollte Michelangelo in einem Brief daran erinnern, „gegen meinen Willen mit größter Gewalt von Papst Paul in die Bauhütte gestellt" worden zu sein. Sein Widerstreben war gerechtfertigt: Der Künstler war mittlerweile über 70 Jahre alt, besaß nur sehr geringe Bauerfahrung und hatte Sangallo, den er für einen mittelmäßigen, wenn auch korrekten, Architekturfachmann gehalten hatte, nie geschätzt; außerdem hatte er zu dem Bauunternehmen, das von Schülern, Mitarbeitern und sogar Familienangehörigen Sangallos geleitet wurde, kein Vertrauen. Die Existenz des so kostspieligen Holzmodells war eine Garantie für Kontinuität und machte weitere Änderungen unwahrscheinlich. Und dennoch konnte er die Aufgabe nicht ablehnen, denn er empfand das Problem von St. Peter als sein persönliches, religiöses Problem. Er stand den katholischen Reformern nahe und hatte sich immer fern von der Kurie gehalten. Mit St. Peter nahm er auf sich und sein Gewissen nicht so sehr das Problem der Darstellung der Rolle des Papstes, sondern der Kirche, so wie er im Jüngsten Gericht ein anderes Problem behandelt hatte, das die Seelen plagte, nämlich die Heilsfrage. Auf der anderen Seite mußte dem Papst bei der Übertragung des Auftrags an Michelangelo bewußt sein, einen tiefen Bruch in der Kontinuität des Bauwerks zu verursachen. Vielmehr mußte er einsehen, daß der große Künstler, der letzte bedeutende eines zu Ende gehenden Zeitalters, der Kunst und nicht mehr der reinen Technik die Aufgabe zurückerstatten konnte, den vor 40 Jahren begonnenen Bauplan endgültig festzulegen. Jetzt wurde die neue Peterskirche erst recht zu einem politischen Problem, indem nicht mehr die Supramatie des Papstes in der Christenheit, sondern die Einheit der Kirche dargestellt werden sollte. Dabei wurde die Kunst zu einer mächtigen Waffe im ideologischen und religiösen Konflikt, der nun ausgebrochen war und für den die Kirche sich ausrüstete.

Anhand des Briefwechsels zwischen Monsignor Archinto, einem der einflußreichsten Mitglieder der Bauhütte, der damals wegen des Konzils in Trient weilte, und seinen römischen Korrespondenten lassen sich die ersten Schritte Michelangelos nachvollziehen. Am 30. November kündigte er zweien der wichtigsten Mitarbeiter Sangallos mit der Begründung, „daß er keinen Menschen, Offizier und Minister aus der Zeit Sangallos wollte". Am folgenden Tag teilte er der Kongregation der Bauhütte mit, daß er in bezug auf das Vorwärtskommen des Bauwerks niemandem außer dem Papst Rechenschaft ablegen wolle. In

deto ordine di Bramante, come à fato il Sangallo, s'è discostato dalla verità; e se così è, chi à ochi non appassionati, nel suo modello può vedere. Lui, con quel circulo che e' fa di fuori, la prima cosa toglie tucti i lumi a la pianta di Bramante"). The letter is a sort of systematic manifesto of Michelangelo's new project for St. Peter's, which in only fifteen days and at a cost of twenty-five scudi (compared with the years and the six thousand scudi necessary for Sangallo's) took the form of a small model, probably in clay, followed by another in wood a year later, at the modest cost of eighty-seven scudi. Only the immense trust he had in the elderly and highly venerated Michelangelo, as well as his ostentatious and stubborn certainty, convinced Paul III to demolish the ambulatory built by Sangallo at the cost of a little more than eighty-five thousand scudi. Michelangelo thought this necessary in order to return to the clear and simple form of the original. Above all, he did not want to disperse in the dark lateral ambulatories the concentrated plastic force of the pier-dome relationship which was reinforced by the walls which seemed to strap in the space, unified and made more dramatic by the light falling directly from above, even in the space covered by the smaller domes. Even though he went back to Bramante's central plan, Michelangelo's design tends nevertheless to transform into energy what Bramante had conceived as balanced spatial expansion. Once the basic project had been clarified, and the proceedings of the construction yard revolutionized, construction went on at a fast pace, thanks to the trust placed in him by the pontiffs in office after the death of Paul III in 1549. Once the four Bramantesque piers destined to support the dome had been reinforced, the creation of the drum started, and the internal side of the ambulatories planned by Sangallo on the external wall of the basilica was transformed. In 1557 Buonarroti started to build the hemispherical semidome of the so-called Chapel of the King of France, or the south arm. Born in 1475, the architect was by then over eighty, and could not follow all the work in person. He limited himself to directing the construction yard from his studio, sending to his supervisor Malenotti the drawings necessary for the construction. Because of a misunderstanding in reading one of the drawings, the supervisor made a mistake in executing the centering in wood needed to construct the vault in travertine, arranging the tables in concentric circles, while Michelangelo's idea was to order three single vaults, each with its own center, on the three windows which illuminate the chapel. As a result, it was necessary to demolish what had already been built at great expense and at the loss of almost a year's work. In a tormented letter, Michelangelo confessed to his friend Giorgio Vasari that he would gladly die of shame if he could ("si potessi morire di vergognia e dolore, io non sarei vivo"). Apart from the misunderstanding, the episode shows how necessary the presence of the elderly master in the construction yard was, as well as the obvious impossibility for him to see the final product of his labors. Perhaps for this reason, convinced

jenen Tagen ließ er den Plan Sangallos von dessen Mitarbeitern hervorholen und kritisierte ihn heftig, da er – wie Vasari berichtet – „mit so vielen Vorsprüngen, Ecken und kleinen Teilen eher einem deutschen Werk entsprach als der guten Art der Alten oder der anmutigen und schönen modernen Weise". Am 25. Januar 1547, als er die ratifizierte Auftragsschrift erhielt, wobei er ein Gehalt für sich ablehnte, trat er schließlich den Abgeordneten der Bauhütte gegenüber. Er berief sich auf seine bevorzugte und ausschließliche Beziehung zum Papst und die alleinige Richtungsvorgabe für die Arbeiten seinerseits und schloß, falls man ihn nicht richtig verstanden haben sollte, mit den Worten: „Ich möchte an dem Bau keine Betrügereien und Diebereien haben, und ich meine damit, daß derselbe, der den Travertin verkauft, auch den Vertrag abschließt; und ich will nicht, daß man mit anderem Mörtel, Steinen und Pozzolanerde mauert als dem, was mir zusagt." Michelangelo wollte demnach wie einst Bramante die alleinige Verantwortung übernehmen und die Mitarbeiter Sangallos sowie die Abgeordneten der Bauhütte, die der Korruption verdächtigt wurden, entfernen. Noch 1557 führte er als Rechtfertigung für die Weigerung, Rom zu verlassen, an, daß er „keine Gelegenheit geben wolle, hierher zurückzukehren, um zu stehlen, wie es die Diebe zu tun pflegen und immer noch darauf warten". Michelangelo beanspruchte die Rückkehr zur Klarheit Bramantes auch für den Entwurf. Im Vergleich zum Grundriß Sangallos war der erste Bauplan für St. Peter, so schrieb der gerade eingestellte Künstler, „nicht voller Durcheinander, sondern klar und ebenmäßig, hell und freistehend ... und wurde als schön beurteilt, wie es auch heute noch deutlich wird. So wie man von der erwähnten Ordnung Bramantes abgewichen ist, was Sangallo getan hat, so ist man auch von der Wahrheit abgewichen. Und wenn dem so ist, kann man dies mit unvoreingenommenen Augen an seinem Modell erkennen. Als erstes beseitigt er mit jenem Kreis, den er außen anbringt, das ganze Licht im Plan Bramantes." Der Brief stellt eine Art Richtprogramm des neuen Projekts Michelangelos für die Peterskirche dar, das in nur 14 Tagen für 25 Scudi (im Vergleich dazu hatte Sangallo mehrere Jahre und 6000 Scudi benötigt) in einem kleinen Modell, wahrscheinlich aus Ton, Gestalt annahm. Ein Jahr später wurde ein Holzmodell, das sich auf nur 87 Scudi belief, angefertigt. Einzig das große Vertrauen in den greisen Michelangelo, den Paul III. über alle Maßen verehrte, und seine hartnäckige Selbstsicherheit überzeugten den Papst davon, den Chorumgang Sangallos, der etwas mehr als 85000 Scudi gekostet hatte, abreißen zu lassen. Dies war unumgänglich, wenn man zu der klaren, einfachen Ursprungsform zurückkehren wollte, insbesondere aber, um in den dunklen seitlichen Chorumgängen die konzentrierte plastische Wirkung der Verbindung Pfeiler-Kuppel nicht zu verlieren. Diese plastische Wirkung wurde durch die Wände verstärkt, die den Raum zu umgürten schienen, sie wurde durch das direkte Licht, das von oben hereinfiel, auch im Bereich der Nebenkuppeln gebündelt und dramatisch gestaltet. Auch wenn Michelangelo das Zentralbauprojekt Bramantes aufgriff, versuchte er dennoch, das, was Bramante als ausgewogene räumliche

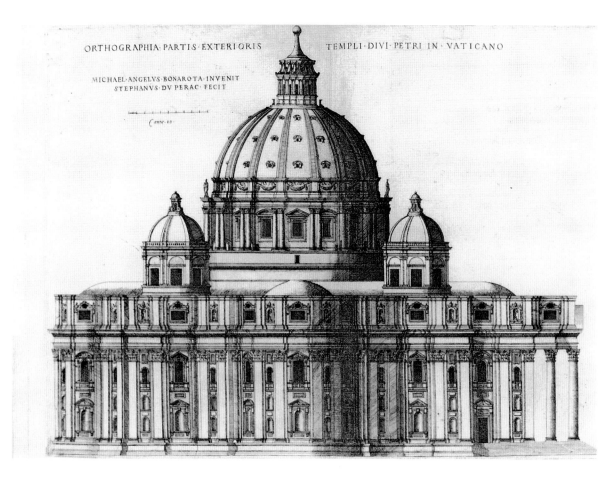

ORTHOGRAPHIA·PARTIS·EXTERIORIS

TEMPLI·DIVI·PETRI·IN·VATICANO

MICHAEL·ANGELVS·BONAROTA·INVENIT
STEPHANVS·DV·PERAC·FECIT

28

**Etienne Dupérac, elevation of the outside of the
project by Michelangelo for St. Peter's**

**Etienne Dupérac, Aufriß der Außenansicht des
Entwurfs Michelangelos für St. Peter**

that he could not change the main dome, he concentrated his last energies in one last heroic effort in defining the form in a big wooden model, which constitutes his last will and testament to the work to which he dedicated such a strenuous effort and the last years of his mortal life. The question of what form to give to the external covering of the dome (which would in any event have been divided, for static reasons, into two different shells) was a real dilemma for Michelangelo. A Florentine who was sufficiently Romanized by that time, he knew well the two possible models – the dome with a raised, almost ogival profile, used by Brunelleschi on the cathedral in Florence, and the hemispherical one of the Pantheon, the ancient temple transformed into a church – and had more than once drawn in pencil (even if we only have the sheets in Lille and in Haarlem) the possible profiles for the covering. The wooden model started in 1558 and finished in 1561, certainly the one still housed in the Vatican, shows a dome with a slightly raised profile, like the one constructed after the death of Michelangelo. But we can be just as sure that the external shell was reworked, at least, if not altogether substituted, in the Sixtine period by Giacomo Della Porta. Dupérac's engravings and reliefs drawn from the model after Michelangelo's death show that his definite choice was for an almost hemispherical external covering, with pronounced double ribs, which correspond to the position of the columns of the drum, lead out of the taut plane interrupted by large windows, almost like a toothed wheel that transforms the heavy mass of the material into

Ausdehnung konzipiert hatte, in Energie umzuwandeln. Nach der Klärung des grundsätzlichen Entwurfs und der Revolution in der Organisationsstruktur machte der Bau zügig Fortschritte, was auch dem ihm entgegengebrachten Vertrauen der Nachfolger Pauls III., der 1549 starb, zu verdanken war. Die vier Pfeiler Bramantes, die die Kuppel tragen sollten, wurden verstärkt und der Bau des Tambours begonnen. Ebenso wandelte man die Innenseite der Chorumgänge Sangallos in die Außenwand der Basilika um. 1557 begann man mit der Ausführung der halbkugelförmigen Nischenwölbung der sogenannten Kapelle des Königs von Frankreich (Cappella del Re di Francia) bzw. dem Südarm. Da Michelangelo 1475 geboren und nunmehr über 80 Jahre alt war, konnte er die Arbeiten nicht persönlich beaufsichtigen, sondern beschränkte sich darauf, das Baugeschehen von seinem Büro aus zu leiten, indem er dem Bauvorsteher Malenotti die notwendigen Zeichnungen zukommen ließ. Aufgrund eines Mißverständnisses bei der Sichtung der Zeichnung ließ der Vorsteher bei der Errichtung des Lehrgerüstes, das für den Bau des Travertingewölbes erforderlich war, fälschlicherweise die Holzbretter in konzentrischen Bögen anordnen. Michelangelo hatte dagegen drei einzelne Gewölbe, jedes mit einem eigenen Mittelpunkt, an den drei Fenstern vorgesehen, die die Kapelle beleuchteten. Demzufolge mußte das bereits Errichtete unter hohem Kostenaufwand wieder beseitigt werden, wodurch mindestens ein Jahr Arbeit verlorenging. Michelangelo gestand seinem Freund Giorgio Vasari in einem qualvollen Brief: „Wenn man vor Scham und Schmerz sterben könnte, wäre ich sicherlich nicht mehr am Leben." Abgesehen von diesem Mißverständnis zeigt die Episode, wie sehr die Anwesenheit des greisen Meisters vonnöten war; zudem schien es ihm unmöglich, seine Mühen beendet zu sehen. Überzeugt davon, die Hauptkuppel nicht mehr errichten zu können, konzentrierte er vielleicht deswegen seine letzten Kräfte mit heldenhafter Anstrengung darauf, die Form in einem großen Holzmodell festzulegen, das sein testamentarisches Erbe für das Werk darstellte, dem er seinen unermüdlichen Einsatz und die letzten Jahre seines Lebens gewidmet hatte. Die Festlegung der Form, die die äußere Schale der Kuppel, die aus statischen Gründen aus zwei Schalen bestehen mußte, annehmen sollte, war für Michelangelo ein großes Dilemma. Als Florentiner, der mittlerweile ein Römer geworden war, kannte er die beiden möglichen Modelle: die Kuppel mit einem gestreckten, fast spitzbogigem Profil, die Brunelleschi über dem Florentiner Dom errichtet hatte, und die halbrunde Kuppel des römischen Pantheons, des antiken, in eine Kirche umgewandelten Tempels. Mit Bleistift hatte er mehrfach die möglichen Kuppelprofile gezeichnet, von denen allerdings nur die Zeichnungen in Lille und Haarlem erhalten sind. Das Holzmodell, das heute noch im Vatikan aufbewahrt wird, wurde 1558 begonnen und 1561 vollendet. Es zeigt eine Kuppel mit leicht gestrecktem Profil wie diejenige, die nach dem Tod Michelangelos ausgeführt wurde. Mit Sicherheit kann man jedoch behaupten, daß die äußere Schale zumindest umgearbeitet, wenn nicht gar völlig in sixtinischer Zeit von Giacomo

vertical thrust. The great outer dome thus summed up, and launched skywards, all of the forces imprisoned in the compressed external walls, which shape an energetically unified organism. Inside, conceived almost like a machine for illumination, it modulated the distribution of light in the great spaces defined not by the abundant decoration of the present day, but almost only by the white surface of the travertine, almost as if the inside had been carved out of a single piece of rock.

That Michelangelo's project was considered unchangeable for many long years can be shown by the unceremonious firing of his immediate successor, the erudite, brilliant and imaginative Pirro Ligorio, who was accused of wanting to distance himself from Michelangelo's ideas, and the assigning of the position in 1573 to the architect who, more than any other, considered himself the heir, interpreter and continuer of Buonarroti's work, Giacomo Della Porta. Without too much ingenuity and with a painful modification of the form of the external crown of the dome, but also with undisputed technical expertise and a respectful lack of ambition, he is nevertheless credited with almost bringing the work of construction to a close. In 1578, he finished the dome of the Gregorian Chapel, then remodelled it with a raised profile to make it harmonize better with the main dome. In 1585, when the choirs of Rossellino and Bramante had been demolished, he closed the covering of the vault of the west arm, the new apse. In 1590 he finished the dome, making the profile higher, and closing it with a new lantern in 1593.

Nevertheless, the change in the form of the dome is not the most significant betrayal of Michelangelo's extraordinary inventions. When the basilica was finished at the beginning of the new century, the east arm was still lacking, in place of the old Constantinian aisle, which was still standing and in use for papal ceremonies. That Michelangelo's project demanded an absolutely central plan is at least as clear to us as it was to all of the "entendeurs" at the end of the Cinquecento. Yet, in 1607, Paul V Borghese decided to open a competition to elongate the longitudinal part of the church – up to the point of covering the soil of the ancient Constantinian basilica – and to work on the façade, since the related drawings by Michelangelo, at least those that were still around at that time (and as far as we are able to know today), were vague and imprecise, so much so as to raise doubts about the fact that he even had a definite project in this respect. The pope's decision to elongate the basilica, and hence to abandon Michelangelo's project, which had, among other things, already been studied by Domenico Fontana for Sixtus V, did not meet with agreement on the part of the entire assembly of the *Fabbrica*. Among the others who, in the name of faithfulness to the ideas of the venerated Florentine artist, were staunchly opposed to abandoning his project was the young, brilliant, learned Monsignor Maffeo Barberini. Undoubtedly, there were many functional and ceremonial pontifical motives for going back to the more

Della Porta ersetzt wurde. Die Stiche Dupéracs und die Aufmaße, die kurz nach dem Tod Michelangelos von dem Modell angefertigt wurden, belegen, daß Michelangelo sich für eine nahezu halbkugelförmige Kuppel entschieden hatte, die stark von doppelten Rippen durchzogen war, die die Säulen des Tambours aufnahmen. Die Säulen waren von der starren Oberfläche des Tambours, die von den großen Fenstern unterbrochen wurde, abgehoben, beinahe wie ein Zahnrad, das die schwere Masse des Materials in vertikalen Druck umwandelt. Die große äußere Kuppelschale faßte auf diese Weise alle Kräfte zusammen, die von den Außenwänden, die einen kraftvoll einheitlichen Organismus formten, ausströmten, und schleuderte sie gen Himmel. Im Innenraum modulierte sie wie ein Beleuchtungsmechanismus die Verteilung des Lichts in den weiten Räumen, die nicht von der heutigen üppigen Dekoration begrenzt wurden, sondern nahezu ausschließlich von der weißen Travertinoberfläche, als ob der Innenraum aus einem einzigen Stein gearbeitet wäre.

Daß der Plan Michelangelos viele Jahre lang als unveränderbar betrachtet wurde, zeigt die plötzliche Kündigung seines direkten Nachfolgers, des gebildeten, meisterhaften und einfallsreichen Pirro Ligorio, der beschuldigt wurde, von den Ideen Michelangelos abweichen zu wollen. Insbesondere aber belegt dies die Tatsache, daß 1573 der Architekt, der als eigentlicher Erbe und Fortsetzer des Werkes Buonarrotis galt, mit der Fortführung beauftragt wurde. Giacomo Della Porta kommt das Verdienst zu, das Bauwerk zwar ohne große Genialität und mit der schmerzlichen Veränderung der äußeren Schalenform der Kuppel, aber mit unbestreitbarem technischen Können und respektvoller Zurückhaltung nahezu zu Ende geführt zu haben. 1578 vollendete er die Kuppel der Gregorianischen Kapelle, die später in eine gestreckte Version umgestaltet wurde, um sie an die Hauptkuppel anzugleichen. Nach dem Abriß des Chores Rossellinos und Bramantes schloß er 1585 die Gewölbedecke der neuen Apsis im Westen. 1590 vollendete er die Kuppel durch die Ansteilung des Gewölbebogens und schloß sie 1593 mit einer Laterne ab.

Die Abwandlung der Kuppelform war dennoch nicht der schlimmste Verrat, der an dem außergewöhnlichen Entwurf Michelangelos begangen wurde. Zur Vollendung der Basilika fehlte zu Beginn des neuen Jahrhunderts noch der Ostarm, der das immer noch stehende alte konstantinische Schiff ersetzen sollte, das für die päpstlichen Zeremonien genutzt wurde. Daß der Entwurf Michelangelos einen Zentralbau vorsah, ist uns heute zumindest so einsichtig, wie es für alle „Experten" Ende des 16. Jahrhunderts war. Und dennoch rief Paul V. 1607 zu einem Wettbewerb auf. Er betraf die Verlängerung der Kirche in Längsrichtung, die sich über die gesamte Fläche der konstantinischen Basilika erstrecken sollte, sowie die Fassade, da die diesbezüglichen Zeichnungen Michelangelos – soweit sie damals erhalten waren und soweit wir heute noch etwas darüber wissen – derartig unklar und ungenau waren, daß Zweifel hinsichtlich ihrer wirklich endgültigen Planung angebracht waren. Der Beschluß des

**Michelangelo, section and elevation of the cupola and lantern of St. Peter's.
Haarlem, Teylers Museum, A29r**

**Michelangelo, Querschnitte und Aufrisse der Kuppel und der Laterne der Peterskirche.
Haarlem, Teylers Museum, A29r**

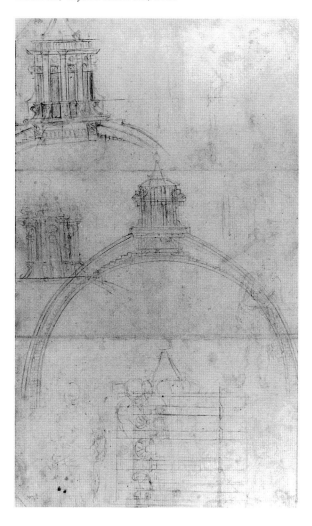

customary longitudinal scheme. For example, the basilica had no baptistery or sacristy, and the connection to the Vatican palace was not ensured. The façade, then, needed a loggia where the the pope could stand and look out over the crowd as he blessed them. Nonetheless, by elongating the nave, Michelangelo's idea would be irremediably compromised. Instead of dominating the entire inside and outside by having the concentrated forces of the members end in a spacious dome, it would fade into the horizon, almost imperceptible.

By grafting a longitudinal body onto the Cyclopean Michelangelesque block, which would thus be reduced to a gigantic tribune, the solemn concept of *templum* (which characterized all of the projects for St. Peter's, to the exclusion of none) was transformed into the more practical one of *ecclesia*, which was more in touch with the spirit of the times. The project chosen was Carlo Maderno's, which was less awkward, and more inclined toward an impossible compromise. Begun between 1608 and 1615, it provided for a visible distinction between an added longitudinal body and the invaded central one. Forced to correct the divine Michelangelo, Maderno did it with remarkable discretion and sensitive criticism. He kept the façade as low as possible, at the limits of the strict rules of the entire tradition, and concentrated his attention on the giant order, which was also derived from Michelangelesque ideas, in order to overshadow the dome as little as possible. Respectfully, he solved the problem, thus satisfying the pontifical request; but he opened others, which kept the architects of the entire seventeenth century busy.

It is significant that, at the end of the Cinquecento, liturgical functionality was to be preferred to faithfulness to a project which had demanded a collective effort of so many generations of architects. The conclusion of the Council of Trent; the beginning of the attempt to reconquer Europe for the Catholic faith; the re-organization of the Church on different bases, with renewed strength derived from the moral regeneration of the community of the faithful and the clergy, are all phenomena which considerably changed the panorama and cultural sensitivity of the period. The religious buildings of the new orders – first and foremost the Jesuits, but also the Theatines and Oratorians – are great halls which were conceived for the purpose of preaching, and for the rites of the crowds of the faithful. The longitudinal scheme is much more suitable to these new demands. At the same time, the controversy against the Lutherans, who favored a relationship with the divine which was not mediated by hierarchy or history, and who openly disputed the cult of the saints, led to the renewed study of ecclesiastical history, to the re-evaluation of the past of the community of the faithful during the late Middle Ages. If it had had to wait until the end of the Cinquecento, the decision to demolish the venerated Constantinian basilica would never have been made at all. Since it was unthinkable to go back on choices already made, at this time when the ancient vestiges were

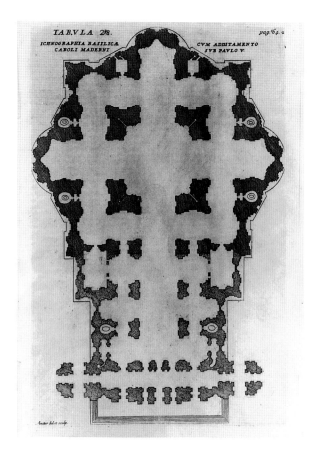

Papstes, die Basilika zu verlängern und damit von dem Vorhaben Michelangelos abzuweichen, was im übrigen schon von Domenico Fontana im Auftrag Sixtus' V. untersucht worden war, wurde nicht von der gesamten Kongregation geteilt. Neben anderen widersetzte sich heftig der junge, gebildete Monsignor Maffeo Barberini, wobei er sich auf die Treue zu den Ideen des verehrten florentinischen Künstlers berief. Zweifelsohne gab es zahlreiche funktionelle bzw. zeremonielle Gründe, zum gebräuchlicheren Längsgrundriß zurückzukehren. Die Basilika besaß beispielsweise kein Baptisterium und keine Sakristei, es existierte auch keine Verbindung zum Vatikanpalast. Die Fassade benötigte zudem eine Loggia, von der aus der Papst seinen Segen erteilen konnte. Dennoch wäre die Idee Michelangelos durch die Verlängerung des Schiffs unwiderruflich beeinträchtigt worden. Statt den gesamten Innenraum mit ihrer Weite zu beherrschen und außen die konzentrierte Kraft der Bauglieder zum Abschluß zu bringen, wäre die Kuppel an den Horizont gerückt und kaum wahrnehmbar gewesen.

Indem an den zyklopisch anmutenden Block Michelangelos ein Längskörper angefügt wurde, ging man von dem feierlichen Templum-Konzept, das bis zu jenem Zeitpunkt ausnahmslos alle Entwürfe für St. Peter gekennzeichnet hatte, zu dem praktischeren und zeitgemäßeren Ecclesia-Konzept über. Die Wahl fiel auf das weniger glückliche Projekt Carlo Madernos, das auf einen unmöglichen Kompromiß abzielte. Der zwischen 1608 und 1615 verwirklichte Entwurf sah eine deutliche Unterscheidung zwischen dem angefügten Längskörper und dem Zentralbau vor. Auch wenn Maderno gezwun-

being destroyed, canons and scholars documented the image, trying to retrace the plan of the old church, copying mosaics and frescoes which would otherwise have been lost. What is more, they tried to save as much as they could manage to detach or take apart with the techniques in use at the time, with so much notarial authenticity certifying the provenance and history of the object. Upon the order of Paul V, ancient sepulchral monuments were placed in the Grottoes, a long space immediately below the level of the new basilica, obtained from the difference between this level and the ancient floor of the Constantinian basilica, later (in 1939) lowered even further. But the new Roman churches gained in ancient marbles and paintings, which were donated by important members of the Curia. In 1596, Clement VIII gave to Duke Lotario II Conti two fragments of the apsidal mosaic from the early years of the thirteenth century. Ten years later, through the generosity of Paul V, the duke's family was able to add the mosaic portrait of their ancestor Gregory IX, from the ancient façade of the church, which had also been destroyed. A head of St. Luke, also from the mosaic of the façade, made its way to the Palazzo Altemps. A Madonna Orante was sent to the church of San Marco in Florence; it was the most important of nine fragments which had been saved from the mosaic decoration of the Oratory of John VII, against the wall inside the façade of the basilica.

It may have been out of a desire to maintain continuity with the ancient decoration of the Early Christian church that, as soon as the dome of the new basilica was finished, it was decided to decorate it with mosaics. The cartoons for these, upon Clement VIII's explicit choice, were executed by Giuseppe Cesari, known as il Cavalier d'Arpino (paid between 1603 and 1612), while the Evangelists of the pendentives were designed just before the Holy Year 1600 by Giovanni de' Vecchi (Saints John and Luke) and by Cesare Nebbia (Saints Mark and Matthew). Once again, the Michelangelesque idea of a space which was defined only architecturally was rejected – but this may have been an element common to the whole of the early Cinquecento. But the choice of the ancient, and unalterable, mosaic technique, which had been out-of-date for some time, marked another phase in the history of the building, which for the first time presented itself as a surface to be sumptuously decorated, like a space to furnish with enormous paintings. At the same time, thanks to the institution of a school of mosaic art, the basilica promoted the re-discovery of a technique that, from the translation of large-scale cartoons for the altarpieces of St. Peter's, would easily continue into the eighteenth century with the minute work of jewelry, the decoration of small panels and snuffboxes, which spread this refined form of high-level artistic craftsmanship expression throughout Europe.

Through an unpredictable incident in history, the young Monsignor Maffeo Barberini, who was opposed to the elongation of the nave decided upon by Paul V, became pope in September 1623. For twenty-one long years,

gen war, den göttlichen Michelangelo zu berichtigen, so tat er dies mit einer bemerkenswerten Zurückhaltung und einer spürbar kritischen Intelligenz. Er hielt die Fassade im Rahmen der strengen Vorschriften und der gesamten Tradition so niedrig wie möglich und richtete seine Aufmerksamkeit auf die Kolossalordnung, die er ebenfalls von Michelangelo ableitete, um die Kuppel möglichst wenig zu verdunkeln. Er löste das Problem respektvoll und stellte den Papst zufrieden. Gleichzeitig schuf er aber neue Probleme, die die Architekten das ganze 17. Jahrhundert hindurch beschäftigen sollten.

Die Tatsache, daß man Ende des 16. Jahrhunderts der liturgischen Funktionalität den Vorzug gab und von einem Projekt, das durch die gemeinsame Anstrengung vieler Architektengenerationen geschaffen worden war, Abstand nahm, ist bezeichnend. Der Abschluß des Trienter Konzils, die Gegenreformation in Europa, die Neuorganisation der Kirche auf unterschiedlichen Ebenen mit neuen Kräften, die die moralische Wiederherstellung der Gemeinschaft der Gläubigen und des Klerus hervorgebracht hatte, all diese Phänomene veränderten spürbar das kulturelle Klima. Bei den Kirchenbauten der neuen Orden, an erster Stelle der Jesuiten, aber auch der Theatiner und Oratorianer, handelte es sich um große Säle, die für die Predigten und die Riten zahlreicher Gläubiger gedacht waren. Dafür war das Längsschema sehr viel geeigneter. Gleichzeitig führte die Polemik gegen die Lutheraner, die eine Beziehung zu Gott ohne die Hierarchien und die Geschichte als Vermittler befürworteten und den Kult der Heiligenverehrung angriffen, zu einem erneuten Studium der Kirchengeschichte und zu einer Wiederaufwertung der frühmittelalterlichen Vergangenheit der Gemeinschaft der Gläubigen. Wenn man gegen Ende des 16. Jahrhunderts die Entscheidung für den Abriß der verehrungswürdigen konstantinischen Basilika hätte treffen sollen, wäre dieser Beschluß vermutlich niemals gefaßt worden. Da man die bereits getroffenen Entscheidungen nicht rückgängig machen konnte, dokumentierten die Kanoniker und Forscher die antiken Überreste zum Zeitpunkt ihrer Zerstörung, vermaßen den Grundriß der alten Kirche und kopierten die Mosaiken und Fresken, die verlorengegangen wären. Man versuchte sogar, alles zu retten, was man mit Hilfe der Technik abnehmen oder auseinanderbauen konnte, und stellte mit notariellen Beurkundungen die Herkunft und die Geschichte der einzelnen Teile fest. Nach dem Beschluß Pauls V. wurden die antiken Grabdenkmäler in den Grotten aufgestellt. Dieser lange, unmittelbar unter dem Niveau der neuen Kirche verlaufende Gang war dank des Höhenunterschieds zwischen der neuen und der alten konstantinischen Kirche ausgegraben worden und wurde 1939 noch tiefer abgesenkt. Aber auch den neuen römischen Kirchen kamen antike Werke aus Marmor und Malereien zugute, die ebenso an bedeutende Vertreter der Kurie verschenkt wurden. 1596 schenkte Clemens VIII. dem Fürsten Lotario Conti II. zwei Mosaikfragmente aus der Apsis, die auf das frühe 13. Jahrhundert zurückgingen. Die Familie des Fürsten konnte diesem Geschenk zehn Jahre später aufgrund der Großzügigkeit

he ruled as Urban VIII. Obviously, he could not demolish what had been constructed in order to correct what had seemed to him to be a serious error. What is more, at the havoc wreaked on Michelangelo's idea, a delicate liturgical problem had to be reckoned with. In fact, by transforming the central scheme of the basilica into a longitudinal one, Paul V had moved the main altar, where the pontiff celebrated the mass, to the apse, as, after all, was the custom in Latin cross churches. But in this way, the location of the papal altar no longer coincided with the tomb of St. Peter, which was placed almost in the center of the dome. In order to emphasize the place where the first of the Apostles was buried, which, without the sacrifice of the mass became something like a reliquary, the Borghese pope had a processional baldachin erected. The work of Ambrogio Buonvicino and Camillo Mariani, it was over nine meters high, in wood, and supported by four angels. In order to emphasize the illusionistic, ephemeral effects, the clothes of the angels and the sky were of real cloth. Immediately below was the stairway which provided access to the tomb. As soon as he was elected, Urban VIII decided to re-unite the two functions that Paul V had rent asunder, and entrusted a promising young sculptor, Gian Lorenzo Bernini, who was barely twenty-five, with the task of creating a bronze baldachin that was also supposed to surmount the papal altar on the tomb of the apostle. The choice of the young sculptor was entirely unexpected, and hence significant: the architect of the construction (from 1603) was still the trustworthy, expert Maderno, who, like his predecessors Vignola and Della Porta, had used the position to become the most important architect of the city. In 1625, Urban VIII himself entrusted Maderno with the job of creating a new, representative palace destined to become the papal family dwelling place. Thus, it was not doubts about his technical capabilities which made the pope prefer the young Bernini to the architect. Moreover, in 1622, it seems as though Maderno had already suggested to the successor of Paul V, the Bolognese Gregorio XV (1621–1623), a solution for transforming the baldachin above the tomb of St. Peter, putting forward the idea of a canopy suspended from on high. In the eyes of Urban VIII, in any event, the question was ambivalent. In fact, by unifying altar and tomb, he also intended to stress Michelangelo's lost centrality, and no one other than the new Michelangelo – or so the precocious Bernini, a true *enfant prodige* of the seventeenth century, was hailed – seemed to him to be capable of bringing such a project to life.

Instead of designing a small architectural piece in marble, which, for however large it might have been, would have seemed miniscule in the grandiose scale of the basilica, Bernini imagined a ceremonial object on a giant scale, thus making an ephemeral object eternal in shining bronze, a processional baldachin in wood and cloth like those which surmounted the pontifical religious functions. In order to create the fantastic object (which, at the time, was defined as a "chimera", a double-headed animal, with the head of a lion and the head of a goat),

Pauls V. ein Mosaikportrait ihres Vorfahren Gregor IX. hinzufügen, das aus der ebenfalls zerstörten antiken Fassade der Kirche stammte. Dem Palazzo Altemps wurde der Kopf des hl. Lukas, ebenfalls aus dem Fassadenmosaik, überlassen. Die Kirche San Marco in Florenz erhielt die Betende Muttergottes, das bedeutendste der neun von der Mosaikdekoration geretteten Fragmente des Oratoriums Johannes' XII., das sich auf der Innenseite der Fassade befand.

Vermutlich um die Kontinuität mit der antiken Dekoration der vorchristlichen Kirche zu bewahren, beschloß man, die Kuppel der neuen Basilika gleich nach dem Abschluß mit Mosaiken auszuschmücken, deren Entwürfe auf ausdrücklichen Wunsch Clemens' VII. von Giuseppe Cesari, dem sogenannten Cavalier d'Arpino, ausgeführt wurden, der zwischen 1603 und 1612 Zahlungen erhielt. Die Evangelisten in den Zwickeln dagegen hatten Giovanni de' Vecchi (Johannes und Lukas) und Cesare Nebbia (Markus und Matthäus) unmittelbar vor dem Heiligen Jahr 1600 entworfen. Wieder einmal verzichtete man auf das Vorhaben Michelangelos, das möglicherweise im gesamten frühen 16. Jahrhundert verfolgt worden war, den Raum ausschließlich architektonisch zu gestalten. Die Wahl der antiken Mosaiktechnik, die seit langem nicht mehr angewandt wurde, stellte einen weiteren Schritt in der Geschichte des Bauwerks dar, das zum ersten Mal als eine prunkvoll zu schmückende Oberfläche erschien, als ein mit riesigen Malereien auszustattender Raum. Dank der Einrichtung einer Schule für Mosaikkunst wurde die Wiederentdeckung einer Technik gefördert, die von der Übertragung der großen Entwürfe auf die Altarbilder in St. Peter rasch zur Feindekoration von Schmuckstücken, kleinen Tischen und Tabakdosen überging, die im 18. Jahrhundert in ganz Europa diese hohe Handwerkskunst verbreiteten.

Durch einen unvorhergesehenen historischen Zufall wurde der junge Monsignor Maffeo Barberini, der sich der von Paul V. beschlossenen Verlängerung des Kirchenschiffs widersetzt hatte, im September 1623 zum Papst gewählt. Als Urban VIII. regierte er 21 Jahre lang. Um den in seinen Augen schwerwiegenden Fehler zu beseitigen, konnte er natürlich das bisher Errichtete nicht wieder abreißen. Außerdem hatte sich neben der Verunstaltung der Idee Michelangelos auch ein prekäres liturgisches Problem ergeben. Durch die Umformung des Zentralbauprojekts in einen Längsbau hatte Paul V. den Hauptaltar in die Apsis verlegt, was in Kirchen, deren Grundriß auf einem lateinischen Kreuz beruhte, üblich war. Auf diese Weise war jedoch die Einheit des Papstaltares mit der Grabstätte Petri, die sich fast genau unter der Kuppelmitte befand, verlorengegangen. Um die Stelle hervorzuheben, an der der Apostelfürst ruhte und die durch die Verschiebung des Altars fast zu einem Reliquiar geworden war, hatte Paul V. einen Prozessionsbaldachin aus Holz errichten lassen, der eine Höhe von über 9 m besaß und von vier Engeln gestützt wurde. Das Werk Ambrogio Buonvicinos und Camillo Marianis besaß zur Betonung seines illusionistischen und vergänglichen Charakters

Bernini combined two different typologies, spiral columns – which are characteristic of the architectural ciborium and refer back to the ancient columns with spiralling shafts in the Constantinian basilica – and the cover with festoons, from which artificial fringe hangs, four great statues of angels holding festive garlands on the corners, thus evoking ephemeral apparatuses set up in St. Peter's for religious feast days. Higher up, the ribs in the form of dolphin's backs, that is, curved like a backwards "S", may have been derived from his intention of referring to another typology, that of the hanging baldachin, as has been conjectured. They constitute an extraordinary conclusion to the bronze apparatus, summing it up and launching it on high, into the great void of the dome, the rotating thrusts originating in the spiral columns, and finally concluding, after having united them at the ends, in the globe surmounted by the cross. Not conceived as a vanishing point in the great central perspective of the nave, but rather as a luminous element that winds into the central space of the basilica, Bernini thought of the baldachin as a form which captures light and distributes it, making it vibrate at the crossing. In this way, he transformed the space imagined by Michelangelo as a moment of supreme balance of all the different tensions at play, into a vital environment where an object emits a strong dynamism with repercussions in the immediate vicinity. In fact, at the same time as the creation of the baldachin, the four great piers which hold up the dome were transformed into colossal reliquaries. To each of the major reliquaries preserved in St. Peter's – the veil of Veronica, on which Christ left the imprint of his face while he was climbing to Calvary; the head of St. Andrew; the lance with which Longinus pierced the side of the Son of God and a fragment of the True Cross – Urban VIII dedicated an altar placed at the base of the pier. Since he had to give architectural form to the transformation of the piers from an element statically determined in a religious place, Bernini articulated them at two different levels of their height. On the upper level, he again took up the form of the spiral column in marble, in order to detach it significantly from the base of a niche which was only slightly hinted at. He thus suggested a greater illusionistic depth than there really was, in the space where the angels showing the holy relics hover. On the lower level, he located four gigantic figures of highly expressive saints in real niches; their pronounced gestures are echoed in the space; they agitate it and put it in immediate relation to the spectator. Thus, for the first time, Bernini conceived of a space in which a highly dramatic action involving the viewer emotionally takes place. The entire crossing – baldachin, piers, loggias, high reliquaries and niches with gigantic statues (one of which, the one representing Longinus, was sculpted by Bernini himself, while he assigned the other three to expert collaborators, the Veronica to Francesco Mochi; the St. Andrew to the young Flemish artist Duquesnoy, the St. Helen to Andrea Bolgi) is imagined as a place whose profound unity is determined by whoever looks at it and moves around in it. It is the initiation of the

Bezüge und einen Himmel aus Stoff. Unmittelbar unter dem Baldachin befand sich die Treppe, die zum Grab hinunterführte. Kurz nach seiner Wahl beschloß Urban VIII., die beiden Funktionen, die Paul V. getrennt hatte, wieder zu vereinen. Er beauftragte Gian Lorenzo Bernini, einen jungen und vielversprechenden Bildhauer, der gerade 25 Jahre alt war, mit der Errichtung eines Bronzebaldachins über dem Apostelgrab, der auch den päpstlichen Altar überdachen sollte. Die Entscheidung zugunsten des jungen Bildhauers kam vollkommen unerwartet und war deshalb von großer Bedeutung. Architekt der Bauhütte (seit 1603) war immer noch der erfahrene und zuverlässige Maderno, der wie seine Vorgänger Vignola und Della Porta sein Amt dazu genutzt hatte, zum wichtigsten Architekten der Stadt aufzusteigen. Urban VIII. hatte Maderno 1625 mit dem Auftrag betraut, einen neuen, repräsentativen Palast als Familienresidenz des Papstes zu erbauen. Der Grund dafür, daß der Papst dem jungen Bernini den Vorzug gab, war also nicht mangelndes Vertrauen in die technischen Fähigkeiten Madernos. Vielmehr schien bereits Maderno 1622 dem Nachfolger Pauls V., dem aus Bologna stammenden Gregor XV. (1621–1923), einen Vorschlag zur Umformung des Baldachins über dem Petrusgrab unterbreitet zu haben, wobei er an einen von oben herabhängenden Baldachin gedacht hatte. Aus der Sicht Urbans VIII. kam diesem Problem eine ambivalente Bedeutung zu. Mit der Vereinigung von Altar und Grab verfolgte er nämlich auch die Absicht, die verlorengegangene Zentralität Michelangelos wiederzubeleben. Kein anderer als der neue Michelangelo, so wurde der frühreife Bernini gefeiert, ein leibhaftiges enfant prodige des 17. Jahrhunderts, schien ihm in der Lage, dieses Vorhaben zu verwirklichen.

Statt ein kleines Marmorbauwerk zu entwerfen, das – auch wenn es noch so groß gewesen wäre – in den gewaltigen Ausmaßen der Basilika sehr klein erschienen wäre, wollte Bernini einen Zeremoniegegenstand gewaltig vergrößern, einen vergänglichen Gegenstand in leuchtender Bronze verewigen, einen Prozessionsbaldachin aus Holz und Stoff wie diejenigen, die bei den Messen des Papstes verwendet wurden. Um diesen Phantasiegegenstand zu verwirklichen, der damals als „eine Chimäre", ein zweiköpfiges Tier mit einem Löwen- und Ziegenhaupt, bezeichnet wurde, kombinierte Bernini zwei verschiedene Typologien miteinander: Die gedrehten Säulen charakterisieren das architektonische Ziborium und erinnern an die antiken Säulen mit dem spiralförmigen Schaft in der konstantinischen Basilika; an den Ecken der Festonendecke, von der künstliche Quasten herabhängen, erheben sich vier große Engelsstatuen, die Festgirlanden hochhalten, was unwillkürlich die Festwagen in Erinnerung rief, die in St. Peter anläßlich der religiösen Feste benutzt wurden. Die weiter oben erkennbaren delphinförmigen Rippen, die wie ein umgekehrtes „S" geschwungen waren, lassen sich vielleicht mit der Typologie des hängenden Baldachins in Zusammenhang bringen, wie häufig vermutet wurde. Vor allem aber stellten diese Rippen einen außergewöhnlichen Abschluß des Bronzeaufbaus dar, indem sie die Aufwärtsbewegung, die durch die gewundenen Säulen

Francesco Borromini, location of the baldachin
in the crossing of St. Peter's.
Vienna, Graphische Sammlung Albertina,
Borromini App. 762

Francesco Borromini, Darstellung des Baldachins
in der Vierung der Peterskirche.
Wien, Graphische Sammlung Albertina,
Borromini App. 762

Baroque that from St. Peter's, at the beginning of the thirties of the seventeenth century (the baldachin was inaugurated in 1633), sparks the transformation of Rome. A collaborator of Bernini, and perhaps the one responsible for the static solution that makes the elegant final crowning element of the baldachin possible, was, in fact, the other great architect of the Roman Baroque period, Francesco Borromini. He was a distant relative of Carlo Maderno, and may have been brought into the construction yard of St. Peter's by his uncle. The young artist first worked as a stonecutter, then draughtsman, and finally architect's assistant. There, he got his training and acquired the technical knowledge which characterize his later career. Rapidly taking distance from Bernini, who was unceremoniously accused of being an ungrateful parasite of the ideas of young, talented artists, Borromini never worked again in St. Peter's, which became the uncontested domain of his rival after 1629. In the basilica, the only things left that he designed are the elegant iron gates which close the Chapel of the Sacrament and the choir.

If, with the baldachin, Bernini managed to transform the inside of the basilica (the regularization of which, from 1645 to 1648, he himself saw to by studying the sheathing of the piers), in the last years of the pontificate of Urban VIII, he attempted to modify the awkward façade of Maderno by adding two bell towers at the ends, according to what Maderno himself had already suggested in 1611. His purpose is clear: the architect wanted a strong front plane, which was airy, transparent, and which would have brought Michelangelo's dome forward – since it was ultimately set behind the low ("quatta", as Bernini called it) façade – by forming a triangle with the bell towers. Once a model in wood had been approved, in November 1636, construction was started on the first of the two bell towers, which were finished in June 1641. But only a few days later, as the contemporary diarist Gigli informs us, part of the tower was destroyed because it was unsatisfactory, and Bernini, having thus been criticized by the pope, became ill and was in danger of dying ("fu disfatto un terzo del detto campanile perché non dava soddisfatione, e il cavalier Bernino che l'aveva fatto fare essendo ripreso dal Papa si ammalò et fu in gran pericolo di morire"). And this is only the beginning of what was to be the most serious professional debacle in Bernini's brilliant career. In fact, when his great protector Urban VIII, who had elevated him to the position of State artist, died, he was succeeded by the enemy of the Barberini, Innocent X, in 1644. It was a time of reckoning for all of the rivals – and there were many – of the ingenious, but all too powerful, cavaliere. His new design for the bell towers was rejected; he had to go on trial under the accusation of technical incompetence because deep cracks resulting from the collapse of the foundations appeared (however, they went back to the period of Maderno); he was humiliated by the demolition of what remained; the travertine left over was used in other construction yards supervised by his rivals. The clock

entstand, bündelten und in den weiten Kuppelraum hochschleuderten und sie schließlich nach der Vereinigung in der Kugel unter dem Kreuz zum Abschluß brachten. Der Baldachin war nicht als Fluchtpunkt der großen Zentralperspektive des Kirchenschiffs konzipiert, sondern als ein lichtvolles Element, das sich in den Hauptkuppelraum der Basilika hineinschraubt. Bernini wollte mit ihm das Licht auffangen und es vibrierend in der Vierung verteilen. Auf diese Weise erzeugte er in dem von Michelangelo entworfenen Raum ein Moment höchsten Gleichgewichts aller verschiedenartigen vorhandenen Spannungen, einen belebten Raum, in dem ein Gegenstand eine starke Bewegung ausstrahlte, die sich in der unmittelbaren Umgebung niederschlug. Zeitgleich mit der Errichtung des Baldachins fand die Umgestaltung der vier mächtigen Kuppelpfeiler in Kolossalreliquiare statt. Urban VIII. weihte jeder der bedeutendsten Reliquien, die in St. Peter aufbewahrt wurden, einen Altar am Fuß der Pfeiler. Die Altäre waren für das sogenannte Schweißtuch der Veronika, auf dem Christus beim Aufstieg nach Golgota seinen Gesichtsabdruck hinterlassen hatte, das Haupt des hl. Andreas, die Lanze, mit der Longinus die Seite des Gottessohnes durchstoßen hatte, und ein Stück des Heiligen Kreuzes bestimmt. Da Bernini den Pfeilern als statisch relevante Elemente in einem Kultort eine architektonische Gestalt geben mußte, unterteilte er sie in zwei unterschiedlich hohe Abschnitte. Im oberen Teil verwendete er in Marmor die Form der Spiralsäule wieder, um sie sichtbar von dem Hintergrund der sonst nur angedeuteten Nische abzuheben. Damit erweckte er den Eindruck einer größeren Tiefe, in der Engel mit den verehrungswürdigen Reliquien wogten. Im unteren Bereich stellte er vier große und sehr ausdrucksvolle Heiligenfiguren in Nischen, deren ausgeprägte Gestik sich im Raum widerspiegelte, ihn in Bewegung versetzte und in eine direkte Beziehung zum Betrachter trat. Zum ersten Mal gestaltete Bernini somit einen Raum, in dem sich eine stark dramatische Handlung abspielte, die auch den Betrachter gefühlsmäßig miteinbezog. Die gesamte Vierung mit dem Baldachin, den Pfeilern, den Reliquien und den Nischen mit den riesigen Statuen, von denen der Longinus von Bernini selbst stammte, während die anderen drei von seinen erfahrenen Mitarbeitern angefertigt wurden (Veronika von Francesco Mochi, der hl. Andreas von dem jungen Flamen Duquesnoy und die hl. Helene von Andrea Bolgi) – diese Vierung wurde als ein Ort konzipiert, dessen tiefgreifende Einheit von dem Betrachter, der sich in ihm bewegte, bestimmt wurde. Dies war der Beginn des Barock, der von St. Peter zu Beginn der 30er Jahre des 17. Jahrhunderts (der Baldachin wurde 1633 geweiht) seinen Ausgang nahm und die Stadt Rom umgestalten sollte. Ein Mitarbeiter Berninis und vermutlich verantwortlich für die statische Lösung, die die elegante Bekrönung des Baldachins möglich gemacht hatte, war der zweite bedeutende Architekt des römischen Barock, Francesco Borromini, ein entfernter Verwandter Carlo Madernos. Von seinem Onkel war er in das Baugeschehen von St. Peter eingeführt worden, wo er in jungen Jahren zunächst als Steinmetz, dann als Zeichner und schließlich als Architektenassistent aus-

towers at the sides of the façade, with mosaic clock faces by Giuseppe Valadier, were not executed until the end of the eighteenth century.

Bernini was to return to the problem of how to draw attention to the dome ten years later, when, after Innocent X had died, Fabio Chigi rose to the throne of St. Peter with the name of Alexander VII. The new pope, very ambitious, was referred to as having "mal della pietra", that is, being stone-sick, according to a naughty comment of his contemporaries, or the "big buildings pope" ("papa di grande edificazione"), because he was so determined in his building program. He was friends with Bernini, and they were the same age. The pope received him almost every day, discussing Rome and his many projects for the city with the artist. Immediately after his election, the Chigi pope decided to provide a suitable way of access to the Vatican basilica and the papal palace by creating a vast square in the place where there was still a trapezoidal space derived from the medieval portico of the Constantinian basilica. This allowed Bernini to return to the problem of the façade of St. Peter's, which he had tried to solve with the high bell towers. The terms of the problem were clear from the architectural and liturgical-functional points of view: the basilica needed an extensive space for the faithful, who were given the blessing *Urbi et Orbi* (that is, to the city and the world) by the pope on special feast days from the loggia above the entrance to the church or, on other less important occasions, from the balcony of his private quarters in the Vatican palace, which were higher than the basilica, on the right, or north, side. Moreover, the pontiff and his court needed to arrange this entrance so that it would be more consonant with the dignity of the important position of those who came there. Located on the northwest side of the square as it was, it was in a rather awkward position. The faithful who came to church, then, had to be received in a vast, sumptuous space, where they could leave their carriages, and where, if they had the proper social status, they could proceed with their horse-drawn vehicles in a covered space.

From the architectural point of view, the pre-existent structures to take into account were obvious: on the one hand, the obelisk erected in 1586 at the wish of Sixtus V thanks to a technical miracle by Domenico Fontana; on the other, the awkward façade of the basilica, which seemed even more out of proportion by the clearly demonstrated impossibility of erecting the bell towers, whose powerful bases visibly added up to the entire width of the façade. Apart from not being exactly axial, the obelisk and façade were on different levels: the first was much lower, and the second elevated by a stairway. Urbanistically, the basilica was reached by crossing two narrow streets, that of the Borgo Vecchio, slightly toward the left of the entrance of the church, and the Borgo Nuovo, which was aligned with the way of access to the Vatican palace. Both widened just before reaching the church in a small square, called Scossacavalli, and were bound, on the side toward the basilica, by blocks of

gebildet wurde und das technische Wissen erwarb, das seine spätere Laufbahn kennzeichnen sollte. Nachdem er sich sehr bald von Bernini entfernt hatte, den er kleinlich als einen undankbaren Parasiten bezeichnete, der die Ideen junger Talente ausnutze, arbeitete Borromini nie wieder in der Peterskirche, die seit 1629 von seinem Rivalen allein beherrscht wurde. In der Basilika hinterließ er nur die von ihm entworfenen eleganten Gitter, die die Sakraments- und Chorkapelle abschließen.

Bernini war es mit dem Baldachin gelungen, den Innenraum der Basilika umzuwandeln, dem er zwischen 1645 und 1648 ein einheitliches Aussehen verleihen wollte und sich zu diesem Zweck mit der Verkleidung der Pfeiler beschäftigte. In den letzten Jahren des Pontifikats Urbans VIII. versuchte er, die unglückliche Fassade Madernos umzugestalten, indem er an den Seiten zwei Glockentürme anfügte, was auch Maderno schon 1611 vorgeschlagen hatte. Durch die Betonung des luftig und transparent erscheinenden Vordergrunds und die optische Verbindung mit den beiden Türmen in Form eines Dreiecks wollte Bernini die Kuppel Michelangelos, die hinter der niedrigen Fassade (Bernini bezeichnete sie als „geduckt") endgültig zurückgetreten war, nach vorne rücken lassen. Nach der Billigung des ersten Holzmodells im November 1636 begann Bernini mit dem Bau des ersten der beiden Türme, der im Juni 1641 vollendet wurde. Aber nach wenigen Tagen, so berichtet der zeitgenössische Tagebuchschreiber Gigli, „wurde ein Drittel des erwähnten Glockenturms niedergerissen, da er nicht zufrieden stellte, und der Cavalier Bernini, der ihn errichtet hatte, erkrankte nach dem Tadel des Papstes und lief Gefahr zu sterben". Dies waren jedoch nur die Vorzeichen der schlimmsten beruflichen Niederlage in Berninis glänzender Laufbahn. Nach dem Tod Urbans VIII., seines großen Förderers, der ihn zum Staatskünstler ernannt hatte, folgte 1644 Innozenz X. als Papst, ein Feind der Familie Barberini. Nun rechneten alle – und es waren sehr viele – Rivalen mit dem genialen, aber zu mächtigen Cavaliere ab. Sein neuer Entwurf für die Türme wurde abgelehnt, und er mußte sich einem Prozeß unterziehen, bei dem er technischer Inkompetenz angeklagt wurde, da sich aufgrund der Senkung der Fundamente tiefe Risse aufgetan hatten, die allerdings schon auf die Zeit Madernos zurückgingen. Er wurde durch den Abriß der verbliebenen Bauteile gedemütigt. Den gewonnenen Travertin verwendete man für andere Bauwerke, die seinen Rivalen unterstanden. Erst im ausgehenden 18. Jahrhundert wurden an beiden Seiten der Fassade zwei Uhren mit einem Mosaikzifferblatt errichtet, die von Giuseppe Valadier ausgeführt wurden.

Auf das Problem der Kuppel kehrte Bernini zehn Jahre später zurück, als nach dem Tod Innozenz' X. Fabio Chigi unter dem Namen Alexander VII. den päpstlichen Stuhl bestieg. Der neue Papst, ehrgeizig und laut einer boshaften Bemerkung seiner Zeitgenossen an „Steinleiden" erkrankt, wurde aufgrund seiner entschiedenen Bauvorhaben auch als „Papst der großen Bauwerke" bezeichnet. Er war ein Freund und Zeitgenosse Berninis. Nahezu täglich emp-

houses which formed the so-called spine of the Borgo. The urban scale is indispensable in order to understand the choices Bernini made: for the first time since the Belvedere courtyard, designed by Bramante, an artist had to organize such a vast space, confronting the problem of the means of architecture. And he had to be ready to force the limits to obtain a result which could only be unifying.

Winning over obstinate resistance due to the very high estimated cost – not only as far as supplies and skilled labor were concerned, but also because of the necessary expropriation of important buildings to demolish – Alexander VII and Bernini ("disegniamo col Bernino" (plan with Bernini), as the pope made a note in his diary) thought of a spacious square surrounded by simple porticoes, against the opinion of the assembly of the *Fabbrica*, which would have preferred high buildings with porticoes with upper levels on which the vicarages could be placed. The reasons behind this choice are obvious, since it was thought that a portico without a structure above it, but with balustrades and statues at every pilaster ("il portico ... senza fabrica sopra ma co'balaustri e con statue a ogni pilastrino", according to the pope's decision on 13 August, 1656) would have ensured that the view of the palace not be obstructed, and, by way of contrast, would have made the façade seem higher. Numerous plans for the vast square were studied: at first, trapezoidal, then rectangular, and even later, circular.

Finally, at the beginning of 1657, the pope accepted the next and even more costly plan proposed by Bernini: to give the square an oval form, 240 meters wide, and to connect it to the basilica and palace with another trapezoidal square, whose larger side would be formed by the façade. Since he had chosen a colonnade, in fact, it was necessary to fill in the discrepancy in the levels of the obelisk and the façade, and this could not be done with columns of the same architectural order, which could only with difficulty be made to go uphill. Moreover, the trapezoidal progression of the "straight square" ("piazza retta"), delimited by pilasters of the "oblique order" ("ordine obliquo"), whose bases and capitals were inclined, would have in some way masked the linguistic deformity, and hid, from the central point of the square, the extremities of the façade, thus reducing its excessive width. The oval form also made it possible to give the maximum amplitude to the square, and the maximum visibility to the faithful, as Bernini had carefully confirmed in several drawings where he had traced out optical targets, and conceived of a space without a single center – as would have happened if the circle had been chosen – but with two opposite focal points which were equidistant from the obelisk.

Once the form of the porticoes had been established, later studies concerned their structure, that is, if they were to be in one, two or three rows, or if the covering was to be vaulted or flat. In order to decide on this, and other aspects, Bernini had a model made on a scale of 1:1, in wood and canvas, thus actually demonstrating the real

fing er den Architekten und diskutierte mit ihm über Rom und seine zahlreichen Baupläne für die Stadt. Kurz nach seiner Wahl beschloß der Papst, einen würdigen Zugang zur Vatikanbasilika und zum päpstlichen Palast zu schaffen, indem er auf der trapezförmigen Fläche des mittelalterlichen Portikus der konstantinischen Basilika einen weiten Platz anlegen lassen wollte. Dies gab Bernini Gelegenheit, sich erneut mit dem Fassadenproblem zu beschäftigen, das er mit den beiden hohen Türmen vergeblich zu lösen versucht hatte. In architektonischer und liturgischer Hinsicht waren die Voraussetzungen klar: Die Basilika benötigte einen weiten Platz für die Gläubigen, denen der Papst anläßlich bedeutender Festlichkeiten von der Loggia über dem Eingang den Segen Urbi et Orbi (für die Stadt und den Erdkreis) spenden konnte. Bei weniger wichtigen Gelegenheiten sollte dies von dem Balkon seiner Privatresidenz im Vatikanpalast geschehen, der höher als die Basilika auf der rechten, d. h. nördlichen Seite lag. Eine weitere Notwendigkeit des Papstes und seines Hofstaates bestand in der Neugestaltung des Palasteingangs, der sich an der Nordwestseite in einer recht unglücklichen Position befand, um der Bedeutung der Besucher besser zu entsprechen. Zudem sollten die Kirchenbesucher auf einem prunkvollen, weiten Platz empfangen werden, auf dem sie ihre Gefährte abstellen und den sie, je nach Wichtigkeit ihrer Stellung, durch ein Dach geschützt mit ihren Pferdekutschen überqueren konnten.

In architektonischer Hinsicht mußten einige schon bestehende Elemente berücksichtigt werden: auf der einen Seite der Obelisk, der 1586 im Auftrag Sixtus' V. und dank eines technischen Wunders von Domenico Fontana hier aufgestellt worden war, auf der anderen Seite die unglückliche Fassade der Basilika, die nach dem fehlgeschlagenen Bau der Glockentürme, deren mächtige Sockel die Fassade auf ihrer gesamten Breite erdrückten, noch unproportionierter wirkte. Der Obelisk und die durch eine Treppe erhöhte Fassade lagen weder auf einer Achse noch auf derselben Höhe. In städtebaulicher Hinsicht konnte man die Basilika über zwei enge Straßen erreichen. Die Straße vom Borgo Vecchio war etwas links vom Eingang der Kirche gelagert, die vom Borgo Nuovo lag mit dem Eingang des Palastes auf einer Linie. Beide Straßen mündeten kurz vor der Basilika in einen kleinen Platz, die sogenannte Piazza Scossacavalli, die auf der Seite zur Kirche von einer Häuserreihe begrenzt wurde, der sogenannten Spina di Borgo.

Die Veranschaulichung des Lageplans ist zum Verständnis der Entscheidungen Berninis unerläßlich. Zum ersten Mal nach dem von Bramante entworfenen Belvedere-Hof sollte ein Künstler einen so ausgedehnten Platz mit architektonischen Mitteln gestalten, um ein einheitliches Ergebnis auch unter Nötigung derselben Mittel zu erhalten.

Zunächst aber mußten Alexander VII. und Bernini den heftigen Widerstand gegen die äußerst hohen Kosten überwinden, nicht nur für die Beschaffung der Materialien und Arbeitskräfte, sondern auch für die notwendigen Enteignungen der bedeutenden Gebäude, die beseitigt werden mußten. Der Papst und der Architekt ("wir zeichnen

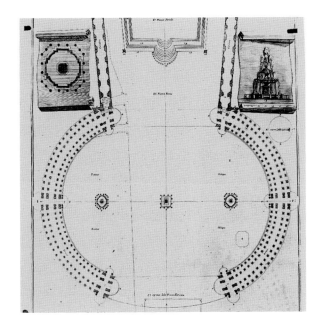

conditions of the view. The project was approved, and on 28 August, 1657, the cornerstone was laid, based on its provisions for a pair of free Corinthian columns surmounted by a straight entablature. But five days later, Bernini presented the pope with another, definitive drawing which substituted the Corinthian columns arranged in pairs with a single, more massive Doric column. In this solution, the one which we see today, there are 284 columns and 88 pilasters, surmounted by an Ionic entablature, arranged in four rows so as to form three lanes. The wider, central lane is for carriages, and covered by a barrel vault; the two lateral ones for pedestrians have coffered ceilings. Above, against the sky, statues of the saints emphatically repeated the same rhythm as the static columns. The alignment of the four columns, carefully studied by Bernini, was done in such a way as to unify the view for the observer in the focal point of the ellipse closer to the resulting semicircle. But, precisely because of this, from the same viewpoint, the view of the opposite semicircle is altogether disorderly, and thus impedes whoever is in the square from having an overall, homogeneous view.

Just as much care had gone into studying the level at which the bases of the columns were to rise from, since they were slightly higher than the level the base of the obelisk rested on in such a way as to make the entrance to the square seem slightly concave and lighten the heavy colonnade. In order to emphasize the horizontal axis, Bernini placed two fountains next to the obelisk (reproducing, on the left, the one already built there in 1613 by Carlo Maderno) and modified the rhythm of the opposite end of the colonnade, thus marking the interruption represented by the lateral accessways.

After this work had begun, Bernini gave the pope another project for the Borgo side: a third arm, which he had first imagined as aligned with the first two, to close the oval, then later slightly pushed back, so as to accentuate the idea of a filter for whoever came from the city. However, the death of Alexander VII in 1667 kept

mit Bernini", schreibt der Papst in seinem Tagebuch) dachten zunächst an einen weiten Platz, der von einfachen Bogengängen gesäumt werden sollte. Die Kongregation sprach sich jedoch dagegen aus und befürwortete stattdessen hohe Gebäude mit einem Portikus, in deren oberen Geschossen die Kanoniker wohnen sollten. Die Gründe für die Wahl waren eindeutig: „Der Portikus (...) ohne Gebäude, aber mit Balustraden und Statuen auf jedem kleinen Pfeiler" (so der Papst am 13. August 1656) hätte die Sicht auf den Palast nicht verdeckt und die Fassade durch den Kontrast höher erscheinen lassen. Es wurden zahlreiche Entwürfe für den weiten Platz angefertigt, der zunächst trapezförmig, später rechteckig und dann wieder rund gestaltet werden sollte.

Schließlich billigte der Papst zu Beginn des Jahres 1657 den noch kostspieligeren Vorschlag Berninis, dem Platz eine ovale Form von 240 m Länge zu geben und ihn mit der Basilika und dem Palast durch einen weiteren, trapezförmigen Platz zu verbinden, dessen breitere Seite mit der Fassade zusammenfallen sollte. Die Wahl der Kolonnade beinhaltete das Problem, den Höhenunterschied zwischen dem Obelisken und der Fassade auszugleichen. Dies konnte jedoch nicht mit Säulen derselben architektonischen Ordnung erreicht werden, die dem ansteigenden Bodenniveau kaum hätten folgen können. Zudem hätte die trapezförmige Gestalt des „geraden Platzes", der von Lisenen der „schrägen Ordnung", bei der die Basen und Kapitelle abgeschrägt wurden, begrenzt wurde, die Veränderung der Formensprache verhüllt und vom Mittelpunkt des Platzes die äußeren Seiten der Fassade verdeckt und ihre Breite reduziert. Die ovale Form gestattete außerdem, dem Platz eine größtmögliche Breite und den Gläubigen eine optimale Sicht zu geben, was Bernini in einigen Zeichnungen mit Perspektivlinien aufmerksam festgehalten hatte. Das Oval sah, im Gegensatz zum Kreis, nicht einen einzigen Mittelpunkt, sondern zwei gegenüberliegende, vom Obelisken gleichweit entfernte Brennpunkte vor.

In weiteren Studien beschäftigte Bernini sich mit der Struktur der Säulengänge. Es mußte festgelegt werden, ob diese aus einem, zwei oder drei Gängen bestehen und ob sie mit einem Gewölbe oder einer flachen Decke abgeschlossen werden sollten. Zu diesem Zweck ließ Bernini mehrere Modelle aus Holz und Tuch im Maßstab 1:1 anfertigen, anhand derer er die tatsächlichen Sichtbedingungen erproben konnte. Am 28. August 1657 wurde schließlich der Grundstein gelegt. Der angenommene Entwurf sah freistehende korinthische Doppelsäulen vor, auf denen ein gerades Gebälk ruhte. Fünf Tage später jedoch legte Bernini dem Papst einen weiteren, diesmal endgültigen Entwurf vor, der die beiden korinthischen Säulen durch eine einzelne, größere dorische Säule ersetzte. Dieser Vorschlag, den wir heute verwirklicht sehen, bestand aus 284 Säulen und 88 Pfeilern mit einem Gebälk ionischer Ordnung. Sie wurden in vier Reihen angeordnet, die drei Gänge bildeten. Der mittlere, breitere Gang war für Kutschen bestimmt und mit einem Gewölbe bedeckt, die beiden äußeren, mit Kassettendecken, für Fußgänger. Die auf der Kolonnade angebrachten Heiligenstatuen

him from bringing it to fruition. But, even without the planned conclusion toward the city, it was only at the end of the thirties of the twentieth century that the unfortunate opening of the via della Conciliazione and the destruction of the "spine" of the Borgo took Bernini's "theater" away from the view. Now, the long perspective of the recent street has pressed it against the façade, thwarting Bernini's studied unity of space.

Every single element in the colonnade was conceived of by Bernini as part of a profoundly unified whole, even at the cost of breaking the rules (mixing the Doric order with the Ionic entablature, the inclination of the capitals and the bases of the pilasters of the two straight arms). Once again, the purpose was the conception of a type of architecture which would create a solemn environment for the spectator, modify the space of the observer, make it permeable, and push the user to explore, by moving around between the two fulcrums, the different possibilities.

Everything was conceived of in relation to the observer, even the remodelling of the Scala Regia, which Bernini certainly thought of in relation – conceptually, before physically – to the colonnade. The task assigned to the architect was clear. It was a matter of the stairway providing access to the Vatican palace: it was narrow, dark and irregular, and its walls tended to converge. Bernini wanted to regularize it, and make it communicate with both the colonnade and the portico of the Vatican basilica.

In the first of the two ramps, immediately after the vestibule which connects it to the portico (in the back of which he sculpted the equestrian statue of Constantine) Bernini placed two rows of slightly converging Corinthian columns. On these, he placed an arch, thus articulating the two walls with pilasters facing each other, and connected to the columns with a straight entablature with shallow niches at intervals. The arch was crowned with two Fames, modelled in white stucco by his brilliant assistant Ercole Ferrata. They hold up the papal coat of arms, thus masking the slight difference between the arch on the columns and the vault of the area. He then split the ramp into two landings, alternating the light sources so that they were either hidden or clearly visible in the coverings, a series of luminous swords that form the successive planes.

Once again, Bernini imagined a space which was constructed entirely for the observer, using perspective not as a rule to measure space with, but to create a sort of reverse telescope, so as to have the observer mentally correct the irregularities which could not otherwise be removed, and persuade the user to ascend.

With the colonnade – which was finished in 1667 – Bernini resolved two problems which were present in the plan for the new St. Peter's from the beginning: the relationship with the city, already established by Maderno and Domenico Fontana (and which, several years later, he was to qualify with the angelic show of the instruments of the passion of Christ on the ancient Pons Aelius,

wiederholten mit Nachdruck gegen den Himmel den Rhythmus der statuenhaft freistehenden Säulen. Bernini arbeitete die Stellung der vier Säulen aufmerksam aus, so daß sich für den Betrachter eine einheitliche Ansicht ergibt, wenn er sich im Brennpunkt der Ellipse, der dem auf diese Weise entstandenen Halbkreis am nächsten liegt, befindet. Gerade aus diesem Grund ist von demselben Standpunkt die Ansicht des gegenüberliegenden Halbkreises vollkommen unklar. Damit hat man von keiner Stelle des Platzes aus eine einheitliche Gesamtsicht.

Ebenso große Aufmerksamkeit schenkte Bernini der Festlegung der Höhenebene, auf der die Säulen emporragen sollten. Sie lag etwas höher als die Ebene, auf der der Sockel des Obelisken stand, und ließ somit den Platz leicht konkav und die schwere Kolonnade höher erscheinen. Zur Betonung der horizontalen Achse stellte Bernini dem Obelisken zwei Brunnen zur Seite, wobei er auf der linken Seite den 1613 von Carlo Maderno errichteten Brunnen nachbildete, und wandelte den Rhythmus der Kolonnade auf der Höhe dieser Achse ab, indem er die Säulenreihen durch seitliche Eingänge unterbrach.

Nach dem Beginn der Bauarbeiten unterbreitete Bernini dem Papst den Vorschlag, auf der Seite des Borgo einen dritten Kolonnadenarm zu errichten, der zunächst gemeinsam mit den anderen beiden das Oval schließen sollte, danach aber leicht zurückversetzt wurde und dadurch für den Besucher, der aus der Richtung der Stadt kam, wie ein Filter wirkte. Der Tod Alexanders VII. im Jahr 1667 verhinderte jedoch die Ausführung. Aber auch ohne den vorgesehenen Abschluß zur Stadt entstellte einzig die unglückliche Anlage der Via della Conciliazione und die Zerstörung der Spina di Borgo Ende der 30er Jahre unseres Jahrhunderts die Ansicht von Berninis „Theater", das die langgestreckte Perspektive der neuen Straße gegen die Fassade gedrängt und damit die Einheitlichkeit des Raums beseitigt hat.

Bernini konzipierte jedes einzelne Element der Kolonnade als Teil eines eng zusammengehörenden Ganzen, auch wenn er dafür durch die Mischung von dorischer Säulenordnung und ionischem Gebälk sowie die Schrägstellung der Kapitelle und der Basen der Lisenen der beiden geraden Arme die Regeln brechen mußte. Ziel war es auch hier, eine Architektur zu konzipieren, die den Betrachter feierlich stimmen und den Raum in seiner Wirkung auf ihn verändern sollte; der Betrachter sollte dazu angehalten werden, die unterschiedlichen Möglichkeiten durch seine wechselnden Standpunkte zwischen den Brennpunkten zu erkunden.

Die Neugestaltung der Scala Regia wurde ebenfalls von der Beziehung zum Betrachter bestimmt. Bernini brachte sie in einen zunächst konzeptionellen und dann auch physischen Zusammenhang mit der Kolonnade. Der Architekt stand vor der Aufgabe, die enge, dunkle und unregelmäßige Eingangstreppe des Vatikanpalastes mit allmählich sich verringernden Abmessungen umzubauen. Sie sollte sowohl mit der Kolonnade als auch mit dem Portikus der Basilika in Beziehung gesetzt werden.

Den ersten der beiden Treppenläufe unmittelbar hinter der Vorhalle, die eine Verbindung zum Portikus herstellte

the only way to get to the basilica), and, thanks to the Scala Regia, the connection with the pontifical palace. In both undertakings, as has been seen, since he could not modify what others had decided upon (the clearing in front of the basilica, the narrow way of access to the old palace), he audaciously used the space to involve the spectator. Before the end of his life, Bernini would in any event have to come to terms with himself. At the same time as the square, in fact, Alexander VII intended to arrange the apsidal end of the basilica in a more fitting manner. In the place where the papal altar had been, he wanted to move a famous relic, one of the most important symbols of pontifical power, the so-called chair of St. Peter, an ivory throne which we now know was probably from the Carolingian period, if not before, but traditionally held to be the seat from which the saint preached to the faithful. The problem that Bernini confronted was twofold: on the one hand, the enormous object could not avoid closing off the view of the basilica; on the other, it could not be situated in such a way as to be the perspectival focal point of the entire nave, annihilating everything Bernini had done up to that time, starting with the crossing. In the earliest drawings of March 1657, he had imagined the chair as located in a niche of dimensions similar to the tombs of Urban VIII and Paul III, almost like an element in relief like the already existent ones. But he soon conceived of a grandiose bronze sheathing decorated with three bas-reliefs – Christ Delivering the Keys to St. Peter, The Washing of the Feet, the Pasce oves meas – held up by the four Church Fathers, two, Augustine and Ambrose, of the Latin Church, and two, John Chrysostom and Athanasius, of the Greek Church. He experimented with this idea first in small sketches (a splendid one related to the chair alone is presently housed in Detroit), then in a model in actual dimensions. Gradually, as work advanced, it became clear that the shining bronze would have been framed by the baldachin. And, it was in studying it in relation to this that he kept enlarging the scale. The attempt to transform the apparatus into pure light is obvious, and even includes the window, surrounding it with golden glory, to the point of merging matter with light, of eliminating the physical closure of the curved apse. Like a vision from beyond this earth, the basilica was not supposed to end in a limit, but in an indefinite, luminous horizon. In place of the vanishing point for the entire basilica, Bernini placed a painted pane of glass with a representation of the Holy Spirit. Up to then, no one had ever gone so far in eliminating the perspectival foundations of architecture. Only in the mystical representation of the small Eucharistic temple, in gilt bronze and lapis lazuli, flanked by two worshipping angels, in the chapel of the Sacrament, Bernini, at the end of his life, almost eighty, expressed in ecstasy the transfiguration of space into light.

All well-contrived, an allegory of the architectural work itself, the new St. Peter's is nonetheless decorated with

und für die Bernini die Reiterstatue Konstantins schuf, versah der Architekt mit zwei sich leicht verjüngenden, korinthischen Säulenreihen, auf denen ein Tonnengewölbe ruhte. Dabei gliederte er die Wände durch Pilaster, die mit den Säulen durch ein gerades Gebälk verbunden waren und in deren Zwischenräumen sich flache Nischen befanden. Bernini krönte den Bogen der Stirnseite des Gewölbes mit zwei Fama-Figuren, die sein hervorragender Assistent Ercole Ferrata aus weißem Stuck angefertigt hatte. Sie halten das Papstwappen und überspielen damit den geringen Unterschied zwischen dem auf Säulen ruhenden Bogen und der Raumwölbung. Er fügte zwei Podeste in die Treppe ein und arbeitete mit zum Teil in der Decke versteckten, zum Teil deutlich sichtbaren Lichtquellen eine Folge von Lichteinfällen aus, die die nachfolgenden Ebenen modellieren.

Auch hier schuf Bernini einen auf den Betrachter abgestimmten Raum, wobei er die Perspektive nicht als Raummaß, sondern als eine Art umgekehrtes Fernglas einsetzte und damit den Betrachter in Gedanken die Unregelmäßigkeiten berichtigen ließ, die auf andere Weise nicht beseitigt werden konnten, so daß er zum Aufstieg bewegt wurde.

Mit der Kolonnade, die 1667 vollendet wurde, löste Bernini zwei Probleme, die bei der Planung der neuen Peterskirche von Anfang an vorhanden waren. Dabei handelte es sich zum einen um die Beziehung zur Stadt, mit der sich bereits Maderno und Domenico Fontana auseinandergesetzt hatten; einige Jahre später klärte Bernini dieses Verhältnis durch die Engelsfiguren und die Leidenswerkzeuge auf dem antiken Pons Aelius, den man überqueren mußte, um zur Basilika zu gelangen. Zum anderen konnte dank der Scala Regia eine Verbindung zum Vatikanpalast hergestellt werden. Da er die Entscheidungen anderer nicht mehr ändern konnte, nutzte er bei beiden Unternehmen entschieden den Raum, um den Betrachter miteinzubeziehen. Gleichzeitig mit dem Platz wollte Alexander VII. die Apsis der Basilika angemessen gestalten und an der Stelle, an der der päpstliche Altar gestanden hatte, eine berühmte Reliquie plazieren sowie eines der bedeutendsten Symbole der päpstlichen Macht, die sogenannte Cathedra Petri, einen Elfenbeinthron, der nach heutigen Erkenntnissen vermutlich aus karolingischer, wenn nicht sogar aus noch früherer Zeit stammt. Der Überlieferung nach soll Petrus von diesem Thron aus den Gläubigen gepredigt haben. Bernini stellte sich nun ein zweifaches Problem: Einerseits mußte das mächtige Werk notgedrungen die Sicht in der Basilika behindern, andererseits durfte es aber nicht zum Fluchtpunkt des gesamten Kirchenschiffs werden, womit all das, was Bernini selbst, von der Vierung angefangen, bisher verwirklicht hatte, zunichte gemacht worden wäre. In den ersten Zeichnungen vom März 1657 hatte er den Thron in eine Nische gestellt, die ähnliche Ausmaße wie die Grabmäler Urbans VIII. und Pauls III. aufwies, fast wie ein gleichwertiges Element. Bald danach entwarf er jedoch ein großartiges Bronzegehäuse, das mit drei Reliefs (Schlüsselübergabe, Fußwaschung, Pasce oves meas) geschmückt war und auf vier

great works of art. Renowned sculptors, the most famous of their times, carried out sepulchral monuments of the popes and of figures of the founders of religious orders in marble, bronze or precious materials in the great niches of the aisles. Famous painters worked out stories and figures for paintings on the altars of the chapels and as decoration for the numerous square meters of the coverings; stonecutters whose names are written down in the registers of the archive of the *Fabbrica* carried out the elegant decoration of the basilica. It would take too long – and might even be pointless – to write even a brief summary: because in St. Peter's, everything is stone. The painting is stone, all translated into the minute tesserae of mosaic, the work of the famous mosaicists of the construction, who succeeded in the impossible job of transmutation, in the patient transformation of the infinite chromatic variations of brushstrokes into stained glass. Even the painted form *par excellence*, the altarpiece, became stone: in 1646, the assembly of the *Fabbrica* commissioned Alessandro Algardi, the highly refined Bolognese sculptor who constituted a dangerous rival to Bernini, to do a large bas-relief of Leo the Great Stopping Attila, a complex scene of many figures, for the altar dedicated to the holy pontiff. In the past, Cavalier d'Arpino and Guido Reni, two of the most brilliant painters of sacred history of the early years of the seventeenth century, had tried their hands at it. For the first time in Rome, sculpture took part in the impalpable quality of painting: in the great model in stucco, which was done on a scale of 1:1 before being transposed into marble, Algardi only managed to ripple the surface, to add up planes which were superimposed one upon the other, making some figures fade into distant depths, and setting them against the figures of the main characters, which are almost in the round – the pope, Attila, the two saints who appear in the sky, and threateningly brandish their swords – with their noble, ancient poses. Why, instead of a painting, commission a complex, gigantic bas-relief, according to a fashion which, for its excessive costs, would have found very few imitators – the pope himself, at the end of the century, the rich religious orders, particularly the Jesuits? And why send, as a gift, as Alexander VII did, the splendid model to the Oratorians who, grateful for the deed, placed it on the stairway of the oratory? In the same way, Clement XI later donated to the poorer churches of the Eternal City, starting with the charterhouse of Santa Maria degli Angeli, the much sought after originals on canvas of the paintings translated into mosaic. Because, at St. Peter's, everything had to be as eternal, as incorruptible as stone, as dazzling as a mosaic.

The element of the eternal which characterizes the decoration at St. Peter's is consciously set against the ephemeral, which has its own privileged place in the basilica. Ever since the early years of the seventeenth century, even before the definitive conclusion of the skeleton of the building, in St. Peter's, the popes had celebrated the rites of canonization, solemn funerals, fires, feast days

Kirchenvätern ruhte, von denen zwei, Augustinus und Ambrosius, aus der lateinischen Kirche, und die beiden anderen, Johannes Chrysostomos und Athanasius, aus der griechischen Kirche stammten. Zunächst fertigte er Bozzetti an, von denen ein wunderschönes Exemplar heute in Detroit aufbewahrt wird, dann ein Modell in Originalgröße. Im Laufe der Arbeit stellte er allerdings fest, daß die leuchtende Bronze vom Baldachin eingerahmt worden wäre. Seine diesbezüglichen Studien führten zu einer zunehmenden Vergrößerung des Maßstabs. Außerdem versuchte er, das Kunstwerk durch die Einfügung eines Fensters in reines Licht umzuwandeln. Er umgab es mit einer vergoldeten Glorie, wobei Materie und Licht eins wurden und der physische Abschluß der Apsis scheinbar beseitigt wurde. Wie bei einer überirdischen Vision durfte die Basilika nicht begrenzt werden, sondern sollte in einem lichtvollen unendlichen Horizont enden. An die Stelle des Fluchtpunkts stellte Bernini eine Glasmalerei, die den Heiligen Geist darstellte. Niemandem war es bisher gelungen, die perspektivischen Grundlagen der Architektur soweit zu beseitigen. Erst in der mystischen Darstellung des Eucharistischen Tempels aus vergoldeter Bronze und Lapislazuli, der sich in der Sakramentskapelle zwischen zwei betenden Engeln befindet, schuf der fast 80jährige Bernini eine ekstatische Verwandlung des Raums in Licht.

Obgleich alles geplant und zugleich Allegorie derselben Planung war, wurde die neue Peterskirche mit außerordentlichen Kunstwerken ausgestattet. Die berühmtesten Bildhauer, die bereits zu Lebzeiten gefeiert wurden, haben aus Marmor, Bronze und wertvollen Materialien Grabmäler für die Päpste oder für die Gründer der Ordensgemeinschaften geschaffen, die in die großen Nischen im Kirchenschiff eingefügt wurden. Bekannte Maler haben Geschichten und Figuren für die Altargemälde in den Kapellen ersonnen und die vielen Quadratmeter der Decke geschmückt. Steinmetze, deren Namen in den Registern des Bauhüttenarchivs erwähnt sind, haben die eleganten Dekorationen der Basilika angefertigt. Selbst eine kurze Zusammenfassung wäre zu umfangreich und vielleicht auch unnütz, denn St. Peter besteht ganz aus Stein. Aus Stein ist die Malerei, die von den berühmten Mosaikmalern der Bauhütte in winzige Mosaikstücke übertragen wurde; ihnen gelang die unmögliche Umwandlung, die geduldige Umsetzung der unendlichen Farbvariationen der Pinselstriche auf farbigem Glas. Aus Stein ist auch das Altargemälde, die gemalte Form schlechthin. 1646 beauftragte die Kongregation der Bauhütte Alessandro Algardi, einen hervorragenden Bildhauer aus Bologna und in jenen Jahren ein gefährlicher Gegenspieler Berninis, mit einem großen Relief, auf dem Leo d. Gr. Attila zurückweist. Diese sehr komplexe Szene mit zahlreichen Personen war für den Altar des Papstes bestimmt. Zuvor hatten sich Cavalier d'Arpino und Guido Reni, zwei der bedeutendsten Maler des frühen 17. Jahrhunderts, daran versucht. Zum ersten Mal teilte die Skulptur die unantastbare Qualität der Malerei. Algardi brach bei dem großen Stuckmodell, das er im Hinblick auf eine spätere Übertragung in Mar-

ALEXANDRI VII PONT MAX MVNVS

mor im Maßstab 1:1 angefertigt hatte, die Oberfläche kaum auf und ließ dadurch übereinandergeschichtete Flächen entstehen, wobei er verschiedene Tiefenebenen abstufte und die Hauptfiguren in ihrer antikisierenden Haltung (den Papst, Attila, zwei Heilige, die mit gezückten Schwertern drohend am Himmel erscheinen) nahezu als Rundplastiken hervorhob. Weshalb wurde statt eines Gemäldes ein riesiges, komplexes Relief in Auftrag gegeben, eine Modeerscheinung, die aufgrund ihrer hohen Kosten nur sehr wenige Nachahmer fand, wie den Papst selbst und gegen Ende des Jahrhunderts die reichen Ordensgemeinschaften, insbesondere die Jesuiten? Weshalb schickte Alexander VII. das herrliche Modell als Geschenk an die Oratorianer, die es dankbar auf der Oratoriumstreppe aufstellten? Weshalb schenkte Clemens XI. später den weniger wohlhabenden Kirchen der Ewigen Stadt, angefangen von der Certosa di Santa Maria degli Angeli, die begehrten Originalleinwände der Gemälde, die in Mosaiken übertragen worden waren? Weil in St. Peter alles ewig sein mußte, unzerstörbar wie Stein, funkelnd wie ein Mosaik.

Das Ewige, das die Dekoration in St. Peter charakterisiert, steht in einem bewußten Gegensatz zum Vergänglichen, das in der Basilika einen besonderen Platz einnimmt. Seit dem frühen 17. Jahrhundert, also noch vor der endgültigen Fertigstellung des Baugerüsts, zelebrierten die Päpste in der Peterskirche Heiligsprechungen, feierliche Bestattungen, Feuerwerke, Feste und Trauerfeiern; es wurden Akte symbolischer politischer Unterwerfung von Herrschern inszeniert, wie beispielsweise die Übergabe des Reitpferdes, eines Schimmels, den der König von Neapel jedes Jahr dem Papst zur Erinnerung an seine Unterwerfung als Geschenk zukommen ließ. Wie für den Platz so wurde auch für die Basilika am häufigsten der Begriff „Theater" verwendet. Die Architekten des Bauwerks waren fast immer experimentelle Regisseure, die geschickten Handwerker nahezu immer in der Lage, ihre Entwürfe in eine vergängliche Beständigkeit, in eine wirkungsvolle und überzeugende Illusion zu übertragen. Und manchmal wurde, wie beim Baldachin, der Cathedra Petri oder der Kolonnade, das Vergängliche in eine Generalprobe umgewandelt, in ein Experiment der gewagtesten bzw. fortschrittlichsten Ideen im Maßstab 1:1.

Die Basilika des Nachfolgers des Apostelfürsten, des Ritus der römischen Päpste, stellt auch heute noch eine einzigartige Szenerie dar. Sie wurde als bedeutendstes Monument der Christenheit konzipiert, als sichtbare Darstellung der legitimen Nachfolge des Fischers aus Galiläa, der nach Rom kam, um als Märtyrer zu sterben. Dennoch ist sie paradoxerweise ein weniger transzendenter Raum, als sich die Architekten jemals vorgestellt hätten, und gleichzeitig der „gesellschaftlichste" Raum des Altertums. Nicht nur weil die Basilika für alle päpstlichen Zeremonien zur Verfügung stehen muß, sondern auch, weil sie im Unterschied zu dem, was Michelangelo dachte, Bernini dagegen aber glaubte und bewies, lehrt, daß man gemeinsam gerettet wird und gemeinsam untergeht.

and mourning, and put on performances of symbolic political submission on the part of rulers, like a sort of homage to the delivery of the Chinea, the white horse which each year was delivered by the King of Naples to the pope in remembrance of his feudal submission. As with the square, the most frequently used term for the Vatican basilica is "theater". The architects of the construction were almost all proven directors. Their skillful workmen were always ready to translate their designs into ephemeral solidity, into effective and convincing illusions. And sometimes – as with the baldachin, or the chair, or the colonnade – the ephemeral was transformed into a dress rehearsal, an experiment with the most daring or advanced ideas on a 1:1 scale.

The basilica of the descendent of the first among the Apostles, of the rite of the Roman pontiffs, is still today the only scenario. Conceived of as the prince of Christianity's monuments, a visible representation of the legitimate descendancy of the fisherman of Galilee who came to Rome to be martyred, St. Peter's is, paradoxically, a space less transcendent than its architects thought it would be. At the same time, it is the most "social" environment of antiquity, not only because it had to be an apparatus available for ritual ceremonies, but because the basilica taught that, contrary to what Michelangelo thought, and instead, as Bernini believed and demonstrated, we are saved together, and lost together.

Alessandro Algardi, model in stucco for the marble altarpiece in St. Peter's representing *St. Leo the Great Stopping Attila*.
Rome, stairway of oratory of the Oratorians

Alessandro Algardi, Stuckmodell für das marmorne Altarbild in der Peterskirche, mit der Darstellung *Leo d. Gr. weist Attila zurück.*
Rom, Treppe im Oratorium der Oratorianer

Chronology

To complete the brief introduction, which essentially concentrated on the architectural vicissitudes of the basilica, the following text will provide the reader with a summarized, chronological list of the decorative work in St. Peter's, from the end of the sixteenth to the end of the eighteenth century, which can still be seen in the church today. Thus, there are no important works of art from the medieval basilica, like the bronze statue of *St. Peter*, the *Tomb of Innocent VIII*, by the Pollaiolo brothers, the bronze doors by Filarete, Michelangelo's *Pietà*, nor works of art (like the altarpieces in slate by Tommaso Laureti, Ludovico Cigoli, Cesare Roncalli, Domenico Passignano, Francesco Vanni, Bernardo Castello, John Baglione commissioned by Clement VIII or those by Poussin, Valentin de Boulogne, or Andrea Sacchi commissioned by Urban VIII) which are no longer in St. Peter's.

1578–1580 After cartoons by G. Muziano, C. Nebbia and P. Manenti, the mosaic decoration of the vault, lunettes and pendentives of the Gregorian Chapel is executed. The only mosaicist named in the documentation in the account books of the *Fabbrica* is G. Caprilli. In a very ruinous state becasue of their age, the pendentive decoration was redone between 1768 and 1772 by the mosaicists L. Fattori, G. B. Fiani, B. Tomberli after cartoons by N. Lapiccola. The decoration of the vault dates from 1772 to 1775, after cartoons by S. Monosilio, by G. B. Fiani and L. Roccheggiani. The decoration of the lunettes between 1776 and 1779, again after cartoons by Lapiccola.
1598–1600 P. Rossetti and L. Martinelli carry out the decoration of the pendentives in the cupola of the crossing, after cartoons by G. De Vecchi (*Sts. John and Luke*), C. Nebbia (*Sts. Matthew and Mark*) and by C. Roncalli (*Angels* and decorative elements).
1600 C. Mariani is paid for the two stucco figures of the *Justice* and the *Fortitude* in the arch on the left of the central nave.
1601–1604 For the decoration of the vault, lunettes and pendentives of the Clementine Chapel, the cartoons by C. Roncalli are converted into mosaics by L. Martinelli, P. Rossetti, M. Provenzale, F. Zucchi, R. Semprevivo, R. Parasoli, D. Parigi.
1603–1612 In the soffit of the dome of the crossing, the cartoons by Cavalier d'Arpino with *Scenes of Christ in Triumph with the Virgin, St. John the Baptist and Apostles* are translated into mosaic by R. Semprevivo, P. Rossetti, C. Rossetti, F. Zucchi, L. Martinelli, D. Parigi, C. Torelli, M. Provenzali; the stucco decoration is executed by R. Solaro.
1612 The thirteen statues of the façade representing *Christ*, the *Baptist* and eleven of the *Apostles* (all of them except St. Peter) are sculpted by E. Moretti, G. Fontana, B. Cennini, S. Drouin, G. A. Valsoldo, C. Fancelli and Braccianese.
1614 A. Buonvicino sculpts the high relief of *Christ Delivering the Keys to St. Peter* on the façade, just below the loggia for the blessing.
Ante 1621 The stucco decoration in the vault of the atrium is finished: the *Acts of the Apostles* is designed by M. Ferrabosco and executed by A. Buonvicino and G. B. Ricci.
1621 The *Tomb of Innocent VIII* (1493–1498), by A. and P. Pollaiolo, is moved to its present location (second pilaster in the left aisle).
1624–1633 Baldachin by G. L. Bernini.
1627–1629 The altarpiece of *St. Michael Archangel* is done in mosaic by G. B. Calandra after a cartoon by Cavalier d'Arpino. Between 1757 and 1758 the altarpiece, the first in mosaic in the new basilica, is substituted by the one by B. Regoli and G. F. Fiani, who translate the *St. Michael* by G. Reni in Santa Maria della Concezione into mosaic; once restored, the mosaic by Calandra is transferred to the cathedral of Macerata in 1771.
1627–1647 *Tomb of Urban VIII* by Bernini.
1628 The *Tomb of Paul III* (1549–1575) by G. della Porta is transferred to its present location.
The wrought iron door of the chapel of the Choir is executed after a model by Borromini.
1628–1631 P. da Cortona paints the *Trinity* for the Chapel of the Sacrament.
1629–1630 The wrought iron door of the Chapel of the Sacrament after Borromini's design, is finished.
1629–1631 G. Lanfranco frescoes the cupola of the Chapel of the Pietà with scenes of the *Exaltation of the Cross* and *Episodes from the Passion.*
1629–1635 After cartoons by G. Lanfranco (*Sts. Bonaventure and Cyril*) and Andrea Sacchi (*Sts. Thomas of Aquinas and John of Damascus*), G. B. Calandra executes the mosaics in the pendentives of the Chapel of the Madonna della Colonna.
1629–1638 Bernini sculpts the *Longinus* for one of the niches in the crossing.
1629–1639 A. Bolgi sculpts the *St. Helen* and F. Duquesnoy the *St. Andrew* for two of the niches of the crossing.
1629–1640 F. Mochi sculpts the *Veronica* for one of the niches of the crossing.
1633–1640 Bernini, together with numerous assistants, finishes the decoration of the loggias, destined to serve as reliquaries, in the piers of the crossing.
1633–1644 Bernini, with the collaboration of different sculptors, carries out the *Monument of Matilde di Canossa.*
1633–1646 Bernini sculpts the *Pasce oves meas* above the door by Filarete.
1634–1652 A. Algardi executes the *Tomb of Leo XI.*
1636–1648 G. B. Calandra and G. U. Abbatini translate into mosaic cartoons by G. F. Romanelli (*St. Gregory Thaumaturge*), C. Pellegrini (*St. Bernard*), A. Sacchi (*Pope Leo and St. Denis*) into mosaic for the pendentives of the Chapel of St. Petronilla and St. Michael.
1640 C. Pellegrini paints the *Martyrdom of St. Maurice*, on the altar to St. Maurice, in the Chapel of the Sacrament.
1643–1647 G. B. Calandra first, and then G. U. Abbatini translate cartoons (1643–1644) by G. F. Romanelli into mosaic for the lunettes of the Chapel of the Madonna della Colonna.
1645–1649 A large group of sculptors and stoneworkers execute the decoration of the piers of the nave, after drawings by Bernini.
1646–1652 A. Algardi sculpts the bas-relief representing *Leo the Great Stopping Attila* for the altar of the Chapel of the Madonna della Colonna and of St. Leo the Great.

Chronologie

Das nachfolgende Gesamtverzeichnis der heute noch vorhandenen Ausstattung der neuen Peterskirche ergänzt die kurze Einführung, die sich im wesentlichen mit der Baugeschichte der Basilika beschäftigt. In chronologischer Reihenfolge sind darin die Werke vom Ende des 16. Jahrhunderts bis zum Ende des 18. Jahrhunderts aufgelistet. Somit werden die bedeutenden Kunstwerke der mittelalterlichen Basilika nicht erwähnt, zu denen beispielweise die Bronzestatue des *Hl. Petrus*, das *Grabmal Innozenz' VIII.* der Pollaiolo, die Bronzetüren Filaretes und die *Pietà* Michelangelos gehören. Ebensowenig wurden die heute nicht mehr in St. Peter vorhandenen Kunstwerke aufgenommen, wie die Altargemälde, die im Auftrag Clemens' VII. nach den Tafeln von Tommaso Laureti, Ludovico Cigoli, Cesare Roncalli, Domenico Passignano, Francesco Vanni, Bernardo Castello und Giovanni Baglione entstanden sind, oder die für Urban VIII. ausgeführten Werke von Nicolas Poussin, Valentin de Boulogne und Andrea Sacchi.

1578–1580 Nach den Kartons von G. Muziano, C. Nebbia und P. Manenti entsteht die Mosaikdekoration im Gewölbe, in den Lünetten und Zwickeln der Gregorianischen Kapelle. Der einzige Mosaikleger, der in den Schriftstücken der Buchhaltung der Bauhütte erwähnt wird, ist G. Caprilli. Die im Laufe der Zeit stark beschädigten Mosaiken in den Zwickeln wurden zwischen 1768 und 1772 nach den Entwürfen N. Lapiccolas von den Mosaiklegern L. Fattori, G. B. Fiani und B. Tomberli erneuert. Die Gewölbedekoration wird zwischen 1772 und 1775 nach den Kartons S. Monosilios von G. B. Fiani und L. Roccheggiani ausgeführt, die Lünettenmosaiken zwischen 1776 und 1779 ebenfalls nach Entwürfen von Lapiccola.
1598–1600 P. Rossetti und L. Martinelli führen die Dekoration in den Zwickeln der Hauptkuppel der Vierung nach den Kartons von G. De Vecchi (*Hl. Johannes* und *Hl. Lukas*), C. Nebbia (*Hl. Matthäus* und *Hl. Markus*) und C. Roncalli (Engel und dekorative Elemente) aus.
1600 C. Mariani erhält ein Entgelt für die beiden Stuckfiguren der *Gerechtigkeit* und des *Starkmuts* am letzten Bogen links im Mittelschiff.
1601–1604 Für die Dekoration des Gewölbes, der Lünetten und der Zwickel in der Clementinischen Kapelle werden die Kartons C. Roncallis von L. Martinelli, P. Rossetti, M. Provenzale, F. Zucchi, R. Semprevivo, R. Parasoli und D. Parigi in Mosaiken umgesetzt.
1603–1612 In der Hauptkuppel der Vierung werden die Kartons von Cavalier d'Arpino mit *Szenen des triumphierenden Christus mit der Jungfrau Maria, Johannes d. T. und den Aposteln* von R. Semprevivo, P. Rossetti, C. Rossetti, F. Zucchi, L. Martinelli, D. Parigi, C. Torelli und M. Provenzali in Mosaiken übertragen. Die Stuckarbeiten stammen von R. Solaro.
1612 Die 13 Statuen an der Fassade, die *Christus, Johannes d. T.* und elf *Apostel* (alle außer dem hl. Petrus) darstellen, werden von E. Moretti, G. Fontana, B. Cennini, S. Drouin, G. A. Valsodo, C. Fancelli und Braccianese ausgeführt.
1614 A. Buonvicino meißelt an der Fassade das Hochrelief der *Schlüsselübergabe*, das sich unmittelbar unter der Segensloggia befindet.
Vor 1621 Die Stuckdekoration des Vorhallengewölbes wird vollendet. Die Apostel werden nach den Ideen M. Ferraboscos von A. Buonvicino und G. B. Ricci ausgeführt.
1621 Das *Grabmal Innozenz' VIII.* (1493–1498), ein Werk A. und E. Pollaiolos, wird an seinem heutigen Standort (zweiter Pfeiler des linken Seitenschiffs) aufgestellt.
1624–1633 Baldachin von G. L. Bernini.
1627–1629 Das Altarmosaik mit dem *Erzengel Michael* wird nach dem Karton des Cavaliers d'Arpino von G. B. Calandra angefertigt. Zwischen 1757 und 1758 wird das erste Mosaik der Basilika durch das Werk von B. Regoli und G. F. Fiani ersetzt, die den *Hl. Michael* von G. Reni in Santa Maria della Concezione in ein Mosaik übertragen. Nach der Restaurierung wird das Mosaik Calandras 1771 in den Dom von Macerata gebracht.
1627–1647 *Grabmal Urbans VIII.* von Bernini.
1628 Das *Grabmal Pauls III.* (1549–1575) von G. della Porta wird an seinem heutigen Standort aufgestellt.
Das Gitter der Chorkapelle entsteht nach den Entwürfen Borrominis.
1628–1631 P. da Cortona malt die *Dreifaltigkeit* für die Sakramentskapelle.
1629–1630 Nach dem Entwurf Borrominis wird das Gitter der Sakramentskapelle angefertigt.
1629–1631 G. Lanfranco führt das Fresko mit Szenen der *Verherrlichung des Kreuzes* und der *Leidensgeschichte* in der Kuppel der Kapelle der Pietà aus.
1629–1635 Nach den Kartons G. Lanfrancos (*Hl. Bonaventura* und *Hl. Cyrillus*) und Andrea Sacchis (*Thomas von Aquin* und *Hl. Johannes von Damaskus*) führt G. B. Calandra die Mosaiken in den Zwickeln der Cappella della Madonna della Colonna aus.
1629–1638 Bernini meißelt die Figur des *Longinus* für eine der Nischen in der Vierung.
1629–1639 A. Bolgi führt die *Hl. Helene* und F. Duquesnoy den *Hl. Andreas* für zwei Nischen in der Vierung aus.
1629–1640 F. Mochi meißelt die Figur der *Veronika* für eine der Nischen in der Vierung.
1633–1640 Bernini arbeitet gemeinsam mit zahlreichen Helfern an der Dekoration der Reliquienloggien an den Vierungspfeilern.
1633–1644 Bernini führt unter Mitarbeit verschiedener Bildhauer das *Denkmal für Mathilde von Canossa* aus.
1633–1646 Bernini meißelt das Relief *Pasce oves meas* über der Tür Filaretes.
1634–1652 *Grabmal Leos XI.* von A. Algardi.
1636–1648 G. B. Calandra und G. U. Abbatini übertragen die Entwürfe von G. F. Romanelli (*Hl. Gregor Thaumaturg*), C. Pellegrini (*Hl. Bernhard*) und A. Sacchi (*Papst Leo* und *Hl. Dionysos*) für die Zwickel der Kapelle der hl. Petronilla und des hl. Michael in Mosaik.
1640 C. Pellegrini malt das *Martyrium des hl. Mauritius* am Mauritiusaltar in der Sakramentskapelle.
1643–1647 Zunächst setzt G. B. Calandra und später G. U. Abbatini die Entwürfe von G. F. Romanelli (1643–1644) für die Lünetten in der

1653–1662 G. U. Abbatini and, after 1656, M. Piccioni, C. Manenti and F. Cristofari transpose cartoons (1652–1667) by P. da Cortona and R. Vanni (lunettes, 1659–1663) into mosaic for the vault, pendentives and lunettes of the Chapel of the Sacrament. The stucco decoration of the vault is by G. Perugino after a drawing by P. da Cortona.
1654–1663 G. U. Abbatini, M. Piccioni, F. Cristofori and O. Manenti decorate the vault, pendentives and lunettes of the Chapel of St. Sebastian in mosaic after drawings (1652–1662) by P. da Cortona with the assistance of C. Ferri (vault, pendentives and two lunettes) and R. Vanni (two lunettes, 1659–1663).
1654–1670 *Equestrian Statue of Constantine*, by Bernini, to the right of the portico.
1655–1678 *Tomb of Alexander VII* by Bernini, with many assistants.
1657–1666 *St. Peter's Chair* by Bernini.
1658–1659 After drawings by Bernini, E. Ferrata does the models for the bronze *Crucifixes* on the altars.
1669–1681 F. Cristofari does the mosaic decoration of the vault (1666–1677), pendentives (1677–1679) and lunettes (1680–1681) in the first bay of the right aisle (Chapel of the Pietà) after drawings by P. da Cortona and C. Ferri.
1672–1678 Altar in the Chapel of the Sacrament, by Bernini.
1675 F. Cristofari, after a drawing by C. Ferri, does the *St. Peter* on the inside of the façade, above the Porta Santa.
1675–1676 Floor of the Chapel of the Sacrament, after a drawing by Bernini.
1681–1703 G. Conti does the mosaic decoration in the pendentives of the Chapel of the Choir, after cartoons (1681–1689 and 1699–1702, respectively) by C. Ferri and C. Maratta.
1682–1689 F. Cristofari translates paintings (1633–1650) by A. Sacchi into mosaic for the altars of the Grottoes (*Veronica; St. Andrew Adoring the Cross He Was Martyred on; Martyrdom of St. Longinus; St. Helen and the Miracle of the True Cross*).
1683–1689 F. Cristofari translates cartoons by Maratta into mosaic for the pendentives and the lunettes of the Chapel of the Presentation.
1685 *Tomb of Clement X*, sculpted by E. Ferrata, G. Mazzuoli, L. Morelli, L. Retti, F. Carcani, F. Aprile, after a design by De Rossi.
1692–1699 The Chapel of the Baptismal Font is carried after a project by C. Fontana; the pool (re-using the upper part of an ancient porphyry sepulchre) is decorated with models by L. Ottoni, J. B. Théodon, M. Maille, and cast by G. Giardini.
1700 *Tomb of Innocent XI*, by P. E. Monnot after a drawing by C. Maratta.
1702 *Monument of Christine of Sweden*, after a drawing by C. Fontana, executed by Théodon e Ottoni.
1704–1725 G. Conti, L. del Pozzo, D. Gossoni, M. Moretti, G. Ottaviani, M. de Rossi, P. Clori translate the cartoons by C. Maratta and G. Chiari into mosaic for the vault of the Chapel of the Conception.
1706–1715 *Tomb of Alexander VIII* after a drawing by C. A. di San Martino, sculpted by A. de' Rossi.
1707 The statues of *St. Elias* (sculpted by A. Cornacchini) and *St. Dominic* (by P. Le Gros) inaugurate the series of Founding Saints located in the niches along the median aisle and the arms of the transept.
1709–1711 F. Cocchi translates into mosaic the *Martyrdom of Sts. Processo and Martiniano*, executed for the central altar of the right transept by V. de Boulogne between 1629 and 1630. Later (1727–1737), the work was completed, or restored, by L. Fattori, G. B. Brughi and P. P. Cristofari.
1711 F. Cristofori does the altarpiece of *St. Nicholas of Bari* in mosaic for the Chapel of the Crucifixion.
1711–1723 G. Ottaviani and P. Clori translate cartoons by M. Franceschini and N. Ricciolini into mosaic for the decoration of the vault and lunettes of the chapel of the choir.
1712–1714 L. Ottoni does the stucco figures of angels for the niches of the drum of the cupola of the Chapel of the Crucifixion, for those of the Chapel of St. Sebastian and the Chapel of the Choir, and for the four corners in the Chapel of the Sacrament.
1716 L. Ottoni does the stucco statues in the large arches providing access to the right transept.
1719 L. Ottoni does the statues in stucco of the popes on the sides of the lunettes of the vault of the atrium.
1719–1723 G. Ottaviani translates cartoons painted by B. Lamberti and, after Lamberti's death, by L. Gramiccia and M. Benefial into mosaic for the lunettes of the Chapel of St. Petronilla and St. Michael.
1720–1725 A. Cornacchini sculpts the equestrian statue of *Charlemagne*, to the left of the portico.
1721–1726 P. P. Cristofari translates the copy (1719–1720) by N. Ricciolini of the *Navicella* painted by Lanfranco in 1631 .
1721–1729 P. Clori, L. Fattori, D. Gossoni, A. Cocchi, G. F. Fiani, E. Enuò do the mosaic decoration in the Chapel of St. Petronilla and St. Michael after cartoons (1721–1726) by N. Ricciolini.
1723 *Tomb of Gregory XIII*, by C. Rusconi and B. Cametti.
1724–1726 L. Fattori, G. Ottaviani, G. B. Brughi translate the cartoons (1713–1723) by F. Trevisani into mosaics for the pendentives of the Chapel of the Baptism.
1725 C. Monaldi sculpts the statue of *St. Francis of Assisi*, from the series of Founder Saints.
L. Ottoni does the stucco cherubs and the angels in the cupola of the Chapel of St. Petronilla and St. Michele.
The two large holy water fonts by G. Lironi, F. Moderati, G. B. De Rossi, A. Cornacchini are placed in their present location.
1725–1727 P. Adami does the *Death of Saphyr*, translating the altarpiece (1599–1604, now in St. Maria degli Angeli) by C. Roncalli into mosaic.
1726–1728 P. P. Cristofari translates into mosaic the cartoon by L. Vanvitelli, a copy of the *Presentation of the Virgin* (1639–1642) by G. F. Romanelli, for the Chapel of the Presentation.
1726–1736 G. B. Brughi and P. P. Cristofari translate *St. Peter Baptizing the Centurion Cornelius* into mosaic for the Chapel of the Baptism after a cartoon (1710–1711) by A. Procaccini.
1726–1738 G. B. Brughi and P. P. Cristofari translate *St. Peter Baptizes Sts. Processo and Martiniano* into mosaic for the Chapel of the Baptism after a cartoon (1709–1711) by G. Passeri.
1728 G. Rusconi sculpts, after a model by C. Rusconi, *St. Ignatius Loyola*, from the series of Founder Saints.

Cappella della Madonna della Colonna in Mosaiken um.
1645–1649 Zahlreiche Bildhauer und Steinmetze arbeiten nach dem Entwurf Berninis an der Pfeilerdekoration im Kirchenschiff.
1646–1652 A. Algardi meißelt für die Cappella della Madonna della Colonna und für die Kapelle Leos d. Gr. das Relief mit der Darstellung *Leo d. Gr. weist Attila zurück*.
1653–1662 G. U. Abbatini und nach 1656 M. Piccioni, C. Manenti und F. Cristofori übertragen die Entwürfe (1652–1667) von P. da Cortona und R. Vanni (Lünetten, 1659–1663) für das Gewölbe, die Zwickel und die Lünetten der Sakramentskapelle in Mosaiken.
1654–1663 G. U. Abbatini, M. Piccioni, F. Cristofari und O. Manenti führen die Mosaikdekoration des Gewölbes, der Zwickel und der Lünetten der Kapelle des hl. Sebastian nach Entwürfen (1652–1662) von P. da Cortona unter Mitarbeit C. Ferris (Gewölbe, Zwickel und zwei Lünetten) und R. Vannis (zwei Lünetten, 1659–1663) aus.
1654–1670 *Reiterstatue Konstantins* von Bernini, rechts neben der Vorhalle.
1655–1678 *Grabmal Alexanders VII.* von Bernini, mit Hilfe zahlreicher Mitarbeiter ausgeführt.
1657–1666 *Cathedra Petri* von Bernini.
1658–1659 E. Ferrata fertigt nach Entwürfen Berninis die Modelle für die Bronzekreuze der Altäre an.
1669–1681 F. Cristofari führt die Mosaikdekoration des Gewölbes (1666–1677), der Zwickel (1677–1679) und der Lünetten (1680–1681) des ersten Jochs des rechten Seitenschiffs (Kapelle der Pietà) nach Entwürfen von P. da Cortona und C. Ferris aus.
1672–1678 Altar der Sakramentskapelle von Bernini.
1675 F. Cristofari führt nach dem Entwurf C. Ferris den *Hl. Petrus* an der Fassadeninnenseite über der Heiligen Pforte aus.
1675–1676 Fußboden der Sakramentskapelle nach Entwürfen von Bernini.
1681–1703 G. Conti führt die Mosaikdekoration der Zwickel der Chorkapelle, nach den Kartons (1681–1689 und 1699–1702) von C. Ferri und C. Maratta aus.
1682–1689 F. Cristofari überträgt die Gemälde (1633–1650) A. Sacchis für die Altäre in den Grotten (*Veronika; Der hl. Andreas betet zum Kreuz seines Martyriums; Martyrium des hl. Longinus; Die hl. Helene und das Wunder des wahren Kreuzes*) in Mosaiken.
1683–1689 F. Cristofari fertigt Mosaiken von den Kartons Marattas für die Zwickel und Lünetten der Cappella della Presentazione an.
1685 *Grabmal Clemens' X.* nach dem Entwurf M. De Rossis, ausgeführt von E. Ferrata, G. Mazzuoli, L. Morelli, L. Retti, F. Carcani und F. Aprile.
1692–1699 Nach Entwürfen C. Fontanas wird die Taufkapelle ausgeführt. Das Taufbecken besteht aus dem oberen Teil eines antiken Porphyrgrabs und wurde mit den von G. Giradini gegossenen Vorlagen von L. Ottoni, J. B. Théodon und M. Maille geschmückt.
1700 *Grabmal Innozenz' XI.* von P. E. Monnot nach dem Entwurf C. Marattas.
1702 *Denkmal für Christine von Schweden*, nach dem Entwurf C. Fontanas von Théodon und Ottoni ausgeführt.
1704–1725 G. Conti, L. del Pozzo, D. Gossoni, M. Moretti, G. Ottaviani, M. de Rossi und P. Clori fertigen nach den Kartons C. Marattas und G. Chiaris für das Gewölbe der Cappella della Concezione Mosaiken an.
1706–1715 *Grabmal Alexanders VIII.* nach Entwürfen von C. A. di San Martino von A. de' Rossi ausgeführt.
1707 Die Statuen des *Hl. Elias* (von A. Cornacchini) und des *Hl. Dominikus* (von P. Le Gros) werden als erste Werke der Reihe der Ordensgründer, die sich in den Nischen des Mittelschiffs und den Seitenarmen des Querschiffs befinden, ausgeführt.
1709–1711 F. Cocchi setzt das *Martyrium des hl. Processus und des hl. Martinianus*, das für den Hauptaltar des rechten Querschiffarms von V. de Boulogne zwischen 1629 und 1630 ausgeführt wurde, in Mosaik um. Später (1727–1737) wurde das Werk von L. Fattori, G. B. Brughi und P. P. Cristofari vervollständigt bzw. restauriert.
1711 F. Cristofori überträgt das Altarbild mit dem *Hl. Nikolaus von Bari* für die Cappella del Crocifisso in Mosaik.
1711–1723 G. Ottaviani und P. Clori fertigen Mosaiken nach den Entwürfen von M. Franceschini und N. Ricciolini für die Dekoration des Gewölbes und der Lünetten der Chorkapelle an.
1712–1714 L. Ottoni führt Stuckengel für die Tambournischen der Kuppel der Cappella del Crocifisso, für die Nischen der Kapelle des hl. Sebastian und der Chorkapelle sowie für die vier Ecken der Sakramentskapelle aus.
1716 L. Ottoni führt die Stuckstatuen an den großen Bogen, durch die man den rechten Querschiffarm betritt, aus.
1719 L. Ottoni führt die Stuckstatuen der Päpste an den Seiten der Lünetten des Vorhallengewölbes aus.
1719–1723 G. Ottaviani setzt die gemalten Vorlagen von B. Lamberti und nach dessen Tod von L. Gramiccia und M. Benefial ausgeführten Entwürfe für die Lünetten der Kapelle der hl. Petronilla und des hl. Michaels in Mosaiken um.
1720–1725 A. Cornacchini führt die *Reiterstatue Karls d. Gr.* links von der Vorhalle aus.
1721–1726 P. P. Cristofari setzt die Kopie (1719–1720) N. Ricciolinis der 1631 von Lanfranco gemalten *Navicella* in Mosaik um.
1721–1729 P. Clori, L. Fattori, D. Gossoni, A. Cocchi, G. F. Fiani und E. Ennuò führen die Mosaikdekoration in der Kuppel der Kapelle der hl. Petronilla und des hl. Michael nach den Kartons (1721–1726) N. Ricciolinis aus.
1723 *Grabmal Gregors XIII.* von C. Rusconi und B. Cametti.
1724–1726 L. Fattori, G. Ottaviani und G. B. Brughi übertragen die Vorlagen (1713–1723) F. Trevisanis für die Zwickel in der Taufkapelle in Mosaiken.
1725 C. Monaldi meißelt die Statue des *Hl. Franz von Assisi* der Reihe der Ordensgründer.
L. Ottoni führt die Stuckcherubim und -engel der Kuppel der Kapelle der hl. Petronilla und des hl. Michael aus.
Die beiden großen Weihwasserbecken von G. Lironi, F. Moderati, G. B. De Rossi und A. Cornacchini werden in der Basilika aufgestellt.
1725–1727 P. Adami fertigt das Mosaik mit dem *Tod der Saphira* nach dem Altargemälde (1599–1604, heute in der Kirche Santa Maria degli Angeli) C. Roncallis an.
1726–1728 P. P. Cristofari setzt den Karton L. Vanvitellis, der *den Tempelgang der Jungfrau Maria*

1728–1730 P. P. Cristofari translates into mosaic the cartoon by S. Conca (1725–1726), a copy of the *Burial of St. Petronilla* executed by Guercino 1623, now in the Pinacoteca Capitolina.

1730 C. Monaldi sculpts the statue of *St. Gaetano Thiene*, from the series of Founder Saints.

1730–1733 P. P. Cristofari translates into mosaic the cartoon painted by L. Vanvitelli, a copy of the *Last Communion of St. Jerome* (1614, now in the Pinacoteca Vaticana) by Domenichino for the altar of St. Jerome in the Gregorian Chapel.

1730–1734 G. B. Brughi and P. P. Cristofari translate a cartoon (paid for between 1696 and 1698) by Maratta of the *Baptism of Christ* into mosaic for the Chapel of the Baptism.

1730–1736 P. P. Cristofari translates into mosaic the cartoon painted by L. Vanvitelli, a copy of the *St. Sebastian* (1625–1635) by Domenichino, from 1736 to St. Maria degli Angeli, for the Chapel of St. Sebastian.

1732 G. B. Maini sculpts *St. Francis de Paul* for the series of Founder Saints.

1735 A. Montauti sculpts *St. Benedict* for the series of Founder Saints.

1736 G. B. Maini sculpts *St. Phillip Neri* for the series of Founder Saints.

1737–1739 P. P. Cristofari translates the altarpiece with the *Martyrdom of St. Erasmus* by Poussin, executed in 1629, into mosaic.

P. P. Cristofari and D. Gossoni translate cartoons by Trevisani into mosaic for the lunettes of the Chapel of the Baptism.

1739–1740 P. P. Cristofari translates the altarpiece of *St. Wenceslas of Bohemia*, executed between 1627 and 1632 by A. Caroselli, into mosaic.

1739–1742 *Tomb of Maria Clementina Sobieski* after a drawing by F. Barigioni, sculpted by P. Bracci; the portrait in mosaic after a drawing by I. Stern is executed by P. P. Cristofari.

1739–1746 P. P. Cristofari, P. L. Ghezzi, E. Ennuò, D. Gossoni, G. F. Fiani, L. Fattori, P. Cardoni, P. Clori, N. Onofri. A. Cocchi translate cartoons (1738–1745) by F. Trevisani into mosaic for the cupola of the Chapel of the Baptism.

1742 P. Campi sculpts *St. Peter Nolasco* for the series of Founder Saints.

1743 M. Slodtz sculpts *St. Bruno* for the series of Founder Saints.

1743–1747 P. Subleyras paints the model with the *Mass of St. Basilius* (now in St. Maria degli Angeli) for the transposition into mosaic of the altarpiece to be located on the altar of St. Basilius (executed between 1748 and 1751, the work of G. Paleat, G. Ottaviani, E. Ennuò, N. Onofri).

1744–1746 N. Onofri, E. Ennuò, G. Ottaviani and G. Paleat translate the painting of P. Bianchi representing the *Immaculate Conception* (1734–1741) into mosaic for the altar of the Chapel of the Choir.

1745 F. della Valle sculpts the *St. Theresa with the Infant Jesus*, and P. Campi the *St. Juliana Falconieri* for the series of Founder Saints.

1746 After a drawing by F. Fuga, Filippo della Valle executes the *Tomb of Innocent XII*.

1749 The *Pietà* sculpted by Michelangelo in 1499 is moved from the Chapel of the Choir to its present location.

1749–1750 G. B. Maini sculpts, under the direction of L. Vanvitelli, the medallions with *Scenes from the Life of Sts. Peter and Paul* in the vaults of the transepts of the tribune.

1751–1753 L. Fattori, D. Gossoni, G. F. Fani, B. Regoli, G. Paleat, G. Ottaviani, P. Polverelli and A. Volpini translate cartoons (1742–1748) by G. Zoboli for the dome of the Chapel of the Madonna della Colonna.

1751–1758 A. Cocchi, E. Ennuò, G. Paleat and G. Ottaviani translate the cartoon by F. Mancini of the *Healing of the Paralytic* (1744–1748) into mosaic for the altar of the Paralytic.

1753 F. Vergara sculpts the *St. Peter of Alcantara*, and P. Pacilli the *St. Camillus de Lellis* for the series of Founder Saints.

1756–1757 After a drawing by C. Marchionni, the jasper base of the bronze statue of *St. Peter* is executed .

1758–1760 G. Ottaviani, G. Paleat, B. Regoli, G. B. Fiani execute the mosaic of the *Resurrection of Tabitha* after a cartoon (1736–1740) by P. Costanzi in place of the painting (1604–1606) by G. Baglione previously on the same altar.

1758–1768 G. F. Fiani, G. Paleat, A. Cocchi, B. Regoli, P. Polverelli, V. Castellini execute, after a cartoon by S. Pozzi (1756–1759), a copy of the *Transfiguration* by Raphael for the altar of the Transfiguration.

1763–1769 *Tomb of Benedict XIV* sculpted by P. Bracci and G. Sibilia (author of the statue of *Self-Denial*).

1770–1772 A. and F. Cocchi and V. Castellini translate a canvas (1625–1627) by A. Sacchi representing *St. Gregory and the Miracle of the Corporal* into a mosaic for the altar of St. Gregory in the Clementine Chapel.

1776–1784 The sacristy is constructed, after a drawing by C. Marchionni.

1784–1792 A. Canova sculpts the *Tomb of Clement XIII*.

1786 G. Valadier places the "big bell" cast by his father Luigi in the the bell tower.

1795–1801 D. Cerasoli, B. Tomberli, F. Cocchi translate into mosaic the cartoon by D. De Angelis representing the *Ecstasy of St. Francis*, based on the painting by Domenichino in Santa Maria della Concezione.

1811–1822 B. Tomberli, V. A. and R. Castellini, R. Cocchi, D. Pennacchini, V. Cocchi, M. Volpini translate into mosaic the cartoon (1806) by V. Camuccini of *The Doubting of St. Thomas*.

1817–1819 A. Canova executes the *Stuart Monument*.

(1639–1642) G. F. Romanellis darstellt, für die Cappella della Presentazione in Mosaik um.

1726–1736 G. B. Brughi und P. P. Cristofari fertigen nach dem Karton (1710–1711) A. Procaccinis ein Mosaik mit dem *Hl. Petrus, der Cornelius tauft* für die Taufkapelle an.

1726–1738 G. B. Brughi und P. P. Cristofari fertigen nach dem Karton (1709–1711) G. Passeris ein Mosaik mit dem *Hl. Petrus, der den hl. Processus und den hl. Martinianus tauft* für die Taufkapelle an.

1728 G. Rusconi führt nach dem Entwurf C. Rusconis den *Hl. Ignatius von Loyola* der Reihe der Ordensgründer aus.

1728–1730 P. P. Cristofari setzt den Karton S. Concas (1725–1726), der Guercinos *Bestattung der hl. Petronilla* (1623, heute in der Kapitolinischen Pinakothek) darstellt, in Mosaik um.

1730 C. Monaldi meißelt die Statue des *Hl. Kajetan von Thiene* der Reihe der Ordensgründer.

1730–1733 P. P. Cristofari fertigt nach dem gemalten Karton L. Vanvitellis, auf dem Domenichinos *Letzte Kommunion des hl. Hieronymus* (1614, heute in der Vatikanischen Pinakothek) dargestellt ist, ein Mosaik für die Gregorianische Kapelle an.

1730–1734 G. B. Brughi und P. P. Cristofari stellen nach dem Karton Marattas (zwischen 1696 und 1698 bezahlt) für die Taufkapelle ein Mosaik mit der *Taufe Christi* her.

1730–1736 P. P. Cristofari setzt den gemalten Karton L. Vanvitellis mit dem *Hl. Sebastian* Domenichinos (1625–1635, seit 1736 in der Kirche Santa Maria degli Angeli) in ein Mosaik für die Kapelle des hl. Sebastian um.

1732 G. B. Maini meißelt den *Hl. Franziskus von Paola* der Reihe der Ordensgründer.

1735 A. Montauti meißelt den *Hl. Benedikt* der Reihe der Ordensgründer.

1736 G. B. Maini meißelt den *Hl. Philippus Neri* der Reihe der Ordensgründer.

1737–1739 P. P. Cristofari führt das Mosaik nach dem Altargemälde Poussins mit dem *Martyrium des hl. Erasmus* (1629) aus.

P. P. Cristofari und D. Gossoni setzen die Kartons Trevisanis für die Lünetten der Taufkapelle in Mosaiken um.

1739–1740 P. P. Cristofari überträgt am Altar des hl. Wenzel von Böhmen das Altargemälde von A. Caroselli (1627–1632) in ein Mosaik.

1739–1742 *Grabmal für Maria Clementina Sobieski* von P. Bracci nach dem Entwurf F. Barigionis. Das Mosaikportrait nach dem Entwurf I. Sterns stammt von P. P. Cristofari.

1739–1746 P. P. Cristofari, P. L. Ghezzi, E. Ennuò, D. Gossoni, G. F. Fiani, L. Fattori, P. Cardoni, P. Clori, N. Onofri und A. Cocchi setzen die Kartons (1738–1745) F. Trevisanis in Mosaiken für die Kuppel der Taufkapelle um.

1742 P. Campi fertigt die Statue des *Hl. Petrus Nolascus* der Reihe der Ordensgründer an.

1743 M. Slodtz meißelt den *Hl. Bruno* der Reihe der Ordensgründer.

1743–1747 P. Subleyras malt die Vorlage mit der *Messe des hl. Basilius* (heute in der Kirche Santa Maria degli Angeli), das in ein Mosaik für den Basilius-Altar übertragen wird (zwischen 1748 und 1751 von G. Paleat, G. Ottaviani, E. Ennuò und N. Onofri ausgeführt).

1744–1746 N. Onofri, E. Ennuò, G. Ottaviani und G. Paleat fertigen nach P. Bianchis Gemälde der *Unbefleckten Empfängnis* (1734–1741) ein Mosaik für den Altar der Chorkapelle an.

1745 F. della Valle führt die *Hl. Theresa mit dem Jesuskind* und P. Campi die *Hl. Juliana Falconieri* der Reihe der Ordensgründer aus.

1746 Nach dem Entwurf F. Fugas führt Filippo della Valle das *Grabmal Innozenz' XII.* aus.

1749 Die 1499 von Michelangelo geschaffene *Pietà* wird von der Chorkapelle an ihren heutigen Standort versetzt.

1749–1750 G. B. Maine führt unter der Leitung L. Vanvitellis die Medaillons mit *Episoden aus dem Leben des hl. Petrus und des hl. Paulus* in den Gewölben der Querschiffarme und der Empore aus.

1751–1753 L. Fattori, D. Gossoni, G. F. Fani, B. Regoli, G. Paleat, G. Ottaviani, P. Polverelli und A. Volpini fertigen nach den Vorlagen (1742–1748) G. Zobolis Mosaiken für die Kuppel der Cappella della Madonna alla Colonna an.

1751–1758 A. Cocchi, E. Ennuò, G. Paleat und G. Ottaviani übertragen nach dem Entwurf F. Mancinis für die *Heilung des Gelähmten* (1744–1748) für den Altar des Gelähmten in Mosaik.

1753 F. Vergara meißelt den *Hl. Petrus von Alcantara* und P. Pacilli den *Hl. Camillus von Lellis* der Reihe der Ordensgründer.

1756–1757 Nach dem Entwurf C. Marchionnis wird der Jaspissockel für die Bronzestatue des *Hl. Petrus* angefertigt.

1758–1760 G. Ottaviani, G. Paleat, B. Regoli, G. B. Fiani führen das Mosaik der *Auferstehung Tabitas* nach den Kartons (1736–1740) P. Costanzis aus, das den Platz eines Gemäldes (1604–1606) von G. Baglioni einnimmt, das sich zuvor an diesem Altar befand.

1758–1768 G. F. Fiani, G. Paleat, A. Cocci, B. Regoli, P. Polverelli und V. Castellini erstellen nach der Vorlage S. Pozzis (1756–1759) eine Kopie der *Verklärung Christi* Raffaels für den Altar der Verklärung.

1763–1769 *Grabmal Benedikts XIV.* von P. Bracci und G. Sibilia (Statue der *Uneigennützigkeit*).

1770–1772 A. und F. Cocchi und V. Castellini setzen A. Sacchis Gemälde mit dem *Hl. Gregor und dem Wunder des Tuches* (1625–1627) für den Altar des hl. Gregor in der Clementinischen Kapelle in Mosaik um.

1776–1784 Nach C. Marchionnis Entwurf wird die Sakristei errichtet.

1784–1792 *Grabmal Clemens VIII.* von A. Canova.

1786 G. Valadier bringt am Glockenturm die von Padre Luigi gegossene große Glocke an.

1795–1801 D. Cerasoli, B. Tomberli und F. Cocchi fertigen nach den Entwürfen D. De Angelis mit der *Ekstase des hl. Franziskus*, die auf dem Gemälde Domenichinos in Santa Maria della Concezione beruhen, Mosaiken an.

1811–1822 B. Tomberli, V. A. und R. Castellini, R. Cocchi, D. Pennacchini, V. Cocchi und M. Volpini setzen V. Camuccinis Vorlage (1806) mit dem *Ungläubigen Thomas* in Mosaik um.

1817–1819 A. Canova führt das *Stuart-Denkmal* aus.

Selected Bibliography

The most recent monograph on the basilica is *La basilica di San Pietro*, edited by C. Pietrangeli, Firenze: Nardini, 1989, while an accurate guide-book is G. Delfini Filippi, *Guide del Vaticano. San Pietro. La basilica e la piazza*, Rome: Palombi, 1989 and id., *Guide del Vaticano. San Pietro. La sagrestia. Il tesoro. Le sacre grotte. La cupola. La necropoli*, Rome: Palombi, 1991. A documentary history of the new St. Peter's is in E. Francia, *1505–1606 La costruzione del nuovo San Pietro*, Rome: De Luca, 1977 and in id., *Storia della costruzione del nuovo San Pietro. Da Michelangelo a Bernini*, Rome: De Luca, 1989. On the Vatican area in the classical period cf. F. Coarelli, *Roma, Guida archeologica*, Bari: Laterza, 1981.

On the tomb of the Apostle, excavated at the middle of the twentieth century, cf. R. Krautheimer *et al.*, *Corpus Basilicarum Christianarum Romae*, Vatican City and New York, 1977, V: 165 and ss. (based on excavations of the first half of the century published in B. M. Apollonj Ghetti, A. Ferrua, E. Josi, E. Kirschbaum, *Esplorazioni sotto la Confessione di San Pietro in Vaticano eseguite negli anni 1940–1949*, Vatican City, 1949); M. Guarducci, *Pietro in Vaticano*, Rome: Istituto Poligrafico e Zecca dello Stato, 1983.

On the history of Rome and the Vatican basilica in the Middle Ages, cf. R. Krautheimer, *Rome: Profile of a City, 312–1308*, Princeton and Guilford: Princeton University Press, 1980. On Nicholas V and Rome at the middle of the Quattrocento, cf. C. W. Westfall, *In the Most Perfect Paradise. Alberti, Nicholas V and the Invention of Conscious Urban Planning in Rome, 1447–1455*, University Park and London: Pennsylvania University Press, 1974.

On the history of the construction in the early Cinquecento, the bibliography is infinite: a useful account of the state of the question can be found in *San Pietro che non c'è. Da Bramante a Sangallo il Giovane* (edited by C. Tessari), Milan: Electa, 1996, which reprints recent contributions by A. Bruschi, C. L. Frommel, F. G. Wolff Metternich and C. Thoenes in Italian. On Michelangelo as architect cf. J. S. Ackerman, *The Architecture of Michelangelo*, New York and London: Zwemmer, 1961 and G. C. Argan and B. Contardi, *Michelangelo, Architect*, New York and London: Abrams – Thames and Hudson, 1993. On Maderno and the history of the basilica under Paul V, cf. H. Hibbard, *Carlo Maderno*, London: Zwemmer, 1971, in particular pp. 155–188.

On the medieval decoration of the basilica in the modern period cf. AA. VV., *Fragmenta Picta*, exhibition catalogue, Rome: Argos, 1989. On G. L. Bernini cf. the classic monograph by R. Wittkower, *Gian Lorenzo Bernini, the Sculptor of the Roman Baroque*, Oxford: Phaidon, 1955 (fourth revised edition, London: Phaidon, 1997), to which should be added I. Lavin, *Bernini and the Unity of Visual Arts*, New York: Pierpont Morgan Library of Art, 1980. On the Scala Regia cf. the very recent volume by T. A. Marder, *Bernini's Scala Regia at the Vatican Palace. Architecture, Sculpture and Ritual*, Cambridge, New York and Melbourne 1997. On the colonnade, besides the classic T. K. Kitao, *Circle and Oval in the Square of Saint Peter's. Bernini's Art of Planning*, New York: New York University Press, 1974, cf. M. Birindelli, *Piazza San Pietro*, Rome and Bari: Laterza, 1981 and *Le statue berniniane del colonnato di San Pietro*, edited by V. Martinelli, Rome: De Luca, 1987.

On the papal tombs in St. Peter's, besides a monograph by P. Fehl in publication, cf., Fehl, *Improvisation and the artist's responsibility in St. Peter's Rome: papal tombs by Bernini and Canova*, in *Akten des XXV Internationalen Kongresses für Kunstgeschichte. 9 Sektion: Eröffnungs- und Plenarvorträge*, Vienna, 1985, pp. 111–123.

On the mosaic decoration F. Di Federico, *The Mosaics of Saint Peter's decorating the New Basilica*, University Park, London: Pennsylvania University Press, 1983. On ephemera, cf. M. Fagiolo dell'Arco, *Corpus delle feste a Roma. La festa barocca*, Rome: De Luca, 1997.

Auswahlbibliographie

Die neueste Monographie zur Peterskirche ist das Werk von C. Pietrangeli (Hg.), *La basilica di San Pietro*, Florenz 1989, während der Band von G. Delfini Filippi, *Guide del Vaticano. San Pietro. La basilica e la piazza*, Rom 1989, sowie die *Guide del Vaticano. San Pietro. La sagrestia. Il tesoro. Le sacre grotte. La cupola. La necropoli*, Rom 1991, desselben Autors sorgfältig ausgearbeitete Führer darstellen, die ausführliche Erläuterungen zur Basilika, zum Platz, zur Sakristei, zum Kirchenschatz, zu den Heiligen Grotten, zur Kuppel und Nekropole enthalten. Eine historische Dokumentation der neuen Peterskirche findet sich im Werk von E. Francia, *1505–1606 La costruzione del nuovo San Pietro*, Rom 1977, sowie in der *Storia della costruzione del nuovo San Pietro. Da Michelangelo a Bernini*, Rom 1989, desselben Autors. Zum Vatikan in klassischer Zeit siehe F. Coarelli, *Rom. Ein archäologischer Führer*, Freiburg i. Br., Basel, Wien 1989.

Über das Apostelgrab, das um die Mitte dieses Jahrhunderts ausgegraben wurde, informiert R. Krautheimer u. a., *Corpus Basilicarum Christianarum Romae*, Vatikanstaat, New York 1977, Bd. V, S. 165 ff (das Werk beruht auf den Ausgrabungen aus der ersten Hälfte dieses Jahrhunderts, die B. M. Apollonj Ghetti, A. Ferrua, E. Josi, E. Kirschbaum in den *Esplorazioni sotto la Confessione di San Pietro in Vaticano eseguite negli anni 1940–1949*, Vatikanstaat 1949, veröffentlicht haben); ebenfalls zu diesem Thema siehe M. Guarducci, *Pietro in Vaticano*, Rom 1983.

Zur Geschichte Roms und zur Basilika im Mittelalter siehe R. Krautheimer, *Rom. Schicksal einer Stadt 312–1308*, München 1996. Zu Nikolaus V. und Rom in der Mitte des 15. Jahrhunderts siehe C. W. Westfall, *In the Most Perfect Paradise. Alberti, Nicholas V and the Invention of Conscious Urban Planning in Rome, 1447–1455*, University Park, London 1974.

Zur Geschichte der Bauhütte im frühen 16. Jahrhundert existiert eine äußerst umfangreiche Bibliographie. Eine nützliche Darstellung zur Thematik gibt C. Tessari (Hg.), *San Pietro che non c'è. Da Bramante a Sangallo il Giovane*, Mailand 1996. Zu Michelangelo als Architekt siehe J. S. Ackermann, *The Architecture of Michelangelo*, New York, London 1961, sowie G. C. Argan, B. Contardi, *Michelangelo, Architect*, New York, London 1993. Zu Maderno und zur Geschichte der Basilika unter Paul V. siehe H. Hibbard, *Carlo Maderno*, London 1971, insbesondere S. 155–188.

Zur mittelalterlichen Dekoration der Basilika in moderner Zeit siehe *Fragmenta Picta*, Ausstellungskatalog, Rom 1989. Zu G. L. Bernini siehe die klassische Monographie von R. Wittkower, *Gian Lorenzo Bernini, the Sculptor of the Roman Baroque*, Oxford 1955 (4. überarbeitete Auflage, London 1997), dem das Werk von I. Lavin, *Bernini and the Unity of Visual Arts*, New York 1980, hinzuzufügen ist. Zur Scala Regia siehe das erst kürzlich erschienene Werk von T. A. Marder, *Bernini's Scala Regia at the Vatican Palace. Architecture, Sculpture and Ritual*, Cambridge, New York, Melbourne 1997. Zur Kolonnade sei neben dem Klassiker T. K. Kitao, *Circle and Oval in the Square of Saint Peter's. Bernini's Art of Planning*, New York 1974, das Werk von M. Birindelli, *Ortsbindung.*

Eine architekturkritische Entdeckung: Der Petersplatz des Gianlorenzo Bernini, Braunschweig, Wiesbaden 1987, und *Le statue berniniane del colonnato di San Pietro*, Rom 1987, von V. Martinelli (Hg.) genannt.

Zu den Papstgrabmälern sei in Erwartung der an-ekündigten Monographie von P. Fehl auf den Aufsatz desselben Autors *Improvisation and the artist's responsibiliy in St. Peter's Rome: papal tombs by Bernini and Canova*, in: Akten des XXV Internationalen Kongresses für Kunstgeschichte, 9. Sektion: Eröffnungs- und Plenarvorträge, Wien 1985, S. 111–123, verwiesen.

Zur Mosaikdekoration siehe F. Di Federico, *The Mosaics of Saint Peter's decorating the New Basilica*, University Park, London 1983. Zu den Festkonstruktionen siehe M. Fagiolo dell'Arco, *Corpus delle feste a Roma. La festa barocca*, Rom 1997.

ST. PETER'S

ST. PETER

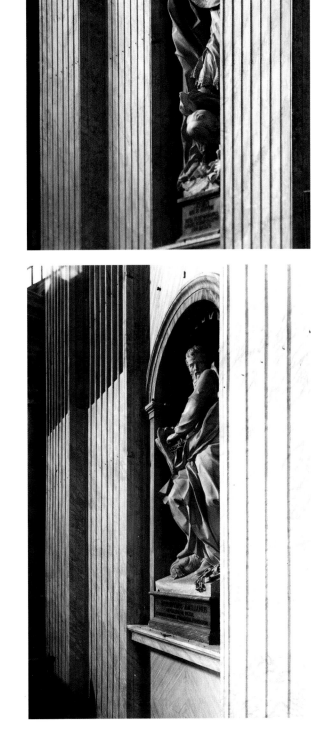

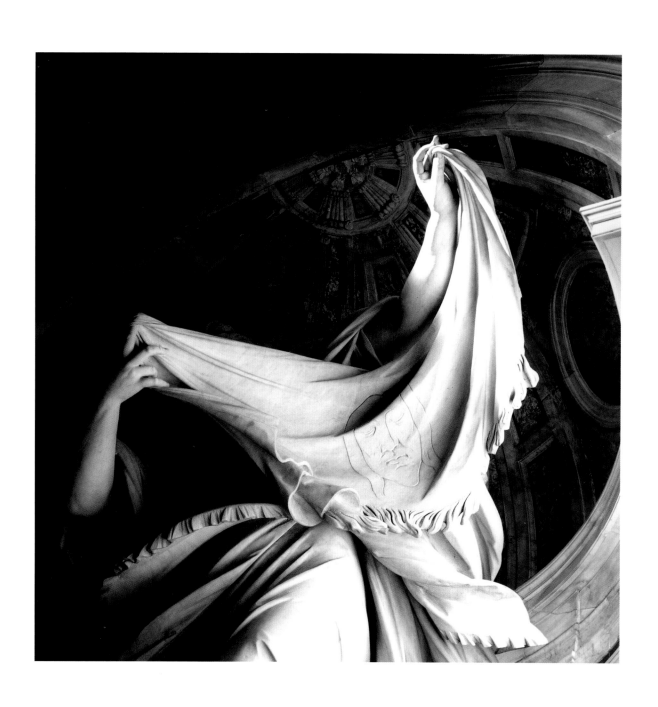

149

Legend

190

Bildlegenden